SAINTLY YOUTH OF MODERN TIMES

SAINTLY YOUTH OF MODERN TIMES

JOAN CARROLL CRUZ

OUR SUNDAY VISITOR PUBLISHING DIVISION
OUR SUNDAY VISITOR, INC.
HUNTINGTON, IN 46750

Our Sunday Visitor Publishing Division
Our Sunday Visitor, Inc.
200 Noll Plaza
Huntington, IN 46750

ISBN-13: 978-1-59276-004-6
ISBN-10: 1-59276-004-X (Inventory No. T59)
LCCN: 2005934904

Cover design by Troy Lefevra
Interior design by Sherri L. Hoffman
Interior photos used with permission

PRINTED IN THE UNITED STATES OF AMERICA

Author's Note

*I*n this book we have a girl, six and a half years old, neither a visionary nor a martyr. Is it possible that she advanced in the spiritual life to such an extent that she can be considered for canonization? What about a child of nine years, another of ten?

After studying the issue for some time, the Vatican concluded that children as young as seven years can, and sometimes do, attain heroic actions of faith, hope, and charity and can be considered for beatification and canonization. In 1981, the Sacred Congregation for the Causes of Saints affirmed this decision with a formal pronouncement to which Pope John Paul II affixed his approval.

So here we have a child only six and a half years old on her way to beatification and canonization, as are all the children mentioned in this book. After reading the history of the Servant of God Antonietta (Nennolina) Meo, six and a half; Venerable Mari Carmen Gonzalez-Valerio, nine years old; and Servant of God Maria a Columna Cimadevilla y Lopez-Doriga, ten years old, one can see that even the very young can attain advanced spirituality.

Then there are the teenagers. Most used modern conveniences, loved music, drove cars, watched TV, went to dances, and talked on the phone with their friends. Almost all died in great pain from dreadful illnesses, some of which endured for years. And all, without exception, had a very deep and active prayer life. Some were martyrs for their faith; some died preserving their purity. All died praising God and fully and joyfully accepting their conditions as being the will of God. Their lives are all different, all extraordinary, all inspiring.

The entries here represent many nations: Brazil, France, Italy, China, Sardinia, Germany, Poland, Spain, Portugal, Mexico, Argentina, Sicily,

Austria, Hungary, Czechoslovakia, and Uganda. Unfortunately, the United States is not represented in this volume. Two saintly children from this country whose names have become familiar — Charlene Richards in Louisiana, and Mary Alice Quinn in Chicago — have cases that have not reached the diocesan level. No investigation into their virtues is currently planned; thus, they are not included here.

We invite readers to examine the index at the back of this book for a list of the occupations or difficulties encountered by these youthful saints. Perhaps you will find someone to whom you can relate, a youthful saint who could become an advocate. We also hope that children now undergoing suffering and hardship can find a measure of comfort and inspiration in the lives of those saintly youngsters who endured similar difficulties.

May these saintly children and teens pray for us, that we, too, will advance in the spiritual life, that we also may accept God's will for whatever troubles may come, and that we will someday enjoy their company in our heavenly homeland.

May God bless us all.

JOAN CARROLL CRUZ

Table of Contents

∽∾∞∾∽

Explanation of Titles

Servant of God: After five years have elapsed since death, and after the bishop of the diocese officially opens the Cause for Beatification, the candidate may be called a *Servant of God.*

Venerable: After the Congregation for the Causes of Saints receives the case, examines it, and determines that the case has merit, a number of preliminary steps are taken. Upon completion of these steps, a *Decree Super Virtutibus* is issued, giving the *Servant of God* the title of *Venerable.*

Blessed: Once a miracle worked through the intercession of the Venerable has been canonically investigated and approved, this, together with the Decree of Heroic Virtues, is passed to the Holy Father, who decides on beatification. After the ceremony of beatification has been held, the Venerable is given the title of *Blessed.*

Saint: For canonization, another miracle performed *after* the beatification ceremony is required. After the miracle has been canonically investigated and approved, the pope may perform a canonization ceremony, and the Blessed is given the title of *Saint.*

A few of the children and teens in this book do not yet have a title. Their cases are in the preliminary diocesan level. Soon, they can be expected to receive the title of *Servant of God.*

Servant of God Albertina Berkenbrock

—⊶⊷—

1919 – 1931
12 years old
BRAZIL

The Brazilian people are anticipating the eventual canonization of this little martyr as their first native-born saint. But her "nationality" really stretches all the way to Germany; her grandparents emigrated to Brazil from Schöppingen, near the town of Münster. When they came to Brazil, they brought with them their three children — one of whom, Johann Hermann, would become the father of our Servant of God.

After Johann married Elisabeth Schmööller, the couple had a large family — nine children. They were a farming family and good Christians who regularly attended church. They recited prayers as a family, especially during May and October when they said special prayers in honor of the Blessed Virgin.

Our little martyr of purity was born on April 11, 1919, in the small village of San Luis, located south of the state of Santa Catarina. She was a beautiful and intelligent child, carefully educated in the faith by her parents. She went to confession frequently and attended Mass regularly, receiving the Holy Eucharist with great fervor. She was to say that the happiest day of her life was the day of her first Holy Communion.

Albertina had great affection for Our Lady, praying fervently to her in the chapel of the church and before the statue in her home. She was also devoted to San Luis, the patron of her church and a model of purity.

Albertina was naturally inclined to goodness, to the practice of religion, and the Christian virtues. She preferred simple amusements and was attracted to the religious life. All things religious pleased her; she was accustomed to making crosses from stray bits of wood found along the roads. She is said to have made many little shrines, decorating them with wildflowers and with pictures of saints given her by the priest.

In her simple, beautiful Christian family, she flourished spiritually. She helped her parents in the fields and in the house. Always docile, obedient, and patient, she calmly endured teasing from her brothers and the boys at school, who loved to taunt her about her shyness, modesty, and repugnance for certain pranks. In such cases, Albertina remained silent, neither rebelled nor sought revenge, and maintained her simplicity and kindness.

She was a delight to her teachers, who considered her spiritually superior to her classmates and of a keen intellect. She applied herself diligently to her studies and knew her Catechism well. She was particularly attracted to the sixth commandment, with its directive to purity and chastity.

Albertina was also charitable, seeking out the poorest girls for her friends, even those who many thought were ethnically inferior. The lunch she brought from home she divided among those who had nothing to eat. She not only knew the virtues but also practiced them to an admirable degree; her teachers, her fellow students, and the adults who knew her esteemed her.

It is not surprising then, that this twelve-year-old girl should meet her unfortunate death in a most heroic manner.

One day, her father's ox was missing, and Albertina was sent into the woods to look for it. She was a beautiful child who appeared much older than her years. This attracted a young man named Idalicio Cipriano Martin (also known as Manuel Martins Da Silva), an employee of her father.

When Manuel saw Albertina walk into the woods alone, he developed a sinful yearning and followed her. He confronted her, but she resisted his request, saying it was a sin that God disliked. When he insisted, she kept repeating that it was a sin that God did not want her to commit. Determined to have his way, he struggled with her and finally threw her to the ground. But Albertina kicked and fought back, and he became enraged. When she began screaming the names of Jesus and Mary, he reached for his penknife and slashed her throat so violently she was almost decapitated. Manuel left the woods terribly spotted with blood, but Albertina's purity had remained intact.

Manuel later confessed to his companions that he wanted to violate Albertina, and that he fully intended to kill her if she resisted. After formally confessing to the crime, he was imprisoned.

The martyrdom of the little virgin of purity transformed the region of San Luis. Pilgrims continually visited her tomb in the parochial cemetery and the place of martyrdom, leaving behind candles and *ex votos* and outlining the site of her martyrdom with stones. The faithful began baptizing babies with the name of Albertina; across the country, some 346 babies were given that name between 1932 and 2000. Eventually, Albertina became so well known that her story came to the attention of the archdiocese, and in 1952, the process of beatification and canonization was begun.

On February 12, 2001, in the cemetery of San Luis, the postulator of her cause, together with Don Hilario Moser, Bishop of Tubarao, had the mortal remains exhumed for the official recognition necessary for the continuation of the process. The remains were then brought into the church in a grand ceremony where they were placed in a sarcophagus of granite constructed in a chapel in the interior of the parish church. This occasion drew an enthusiastic crowd — 5,000 more than expected.

Today, an abundance of candles from devotees illuminate the chapel, and the sacred place never lacks flowers. The place also contains books for registering favors received, as well as those favors awaiting the intercession of the little martyr.

Albertina is the subject of several other books as well. One of the martyr's relatives is listing all the favors received so far, and the many cures that have been studied by physicians. Encouraged by these favors obtained through Albertina's intercession, pilgrims continue to flock to her tomb;in one week, 47 crowded buses arrived, originating from all parts of Brazil.

The Cause of Albertina Berkenbrock awaits the attention of the Vatican, while devoted people of Brazil pray for the eventual beatification and canonization of their little martyr of purity. ✝

Servant of God Aldo Blundo

1919 – 1934
15 years old
ITALY

*B*orn in Naples on January 23, 1919, this candidate for beatification was actually placed under the protection of four saints when he was given the names of Aldo, Francis, Joseph, and Maria. His brief life is said to have been a "pilgrimage of pain which was illuminated by his faith and by his great spirit of prayer . . . an unusual spiritual ascension at his age which was fed by the Eucharist."

From infancy, Aldo was stricken with a variety of infirmities that caused his parents, Paul and Maria Blundo, untold anxiety. Up to the age of five he suffered from pleurisy, bronchitis, pneumonia, and a persistent cough affecting his throat. He had difficulty moving; this, doctors diagnosed as hypertrophy, an abnormal enlargement of the muscles. In Aldo's case, this condition involved the pelvic region, which eventually became paralyzed. In addition to these ailments, he was also diagnosed with eye problems, specifically, progressive degenerate myopia. At the tender age of eight, Aldo already had failing eyesight and was condemned to immobility. Then, after a fall, he suffered a broken leg that failed to heal properly.

At last, Aldo was confined and tied to the bed or a wheelchair, free to move only his head and his hands. Although suffering, he was resigned to his pain and inspired by the Passion of Our Lord. He once openly declared that he was offering his own life for the salvation of sinners. Aldo said that he was prepared to do the will of God and to bear his condition in exchange for the recovery of wayward youth and for the priesthood. His prayers were answered with respect to a Dominican priest who had made his acquaintance. The priest credits Aldo with restoring him to serenity of spirit after he had undergone a lengthy period of spiritual crisis.

Aldo's example of patient suffering and his inspired pronouncements deeply affected his family, especially his father, a non-practicing Catholic. In a well-meaning effort to help his son, he inadvertently added to his suffering by having him undergo painful physical therapy, electrotherapy, and drug therapy, along with other procedures of doubtful efficacy, among them an orthopedic apparatus that caused excruciating pain. Finally, after undergoing these treatments without complaint, the child asked his father, "Why waste so much money? Only the Madonna can help me."

By 1929, when Aldo was ten years old, his family had exhausted all other treatment options and brought him to the shrine of Our Lady of the Rosary in nearby Pompeii. This was followed by a pilgrimage to Lourdes in 1934. When asked how he felt, Aldo continued to answer with a smile, saying, "I am fine, my pains are not so bad." Imprisoned in his own body, Aldo was a model of suffering offered for Jesus and Mary. When the mother's domestic duties permitted, she recited the Holy Rosary with her son; when he was alone, he prayed the Rosary by himself, with his eyes closed in deep meditation.

Aldo was devoted to the Apostolate of Prayer and expressed a desire for his whole family to be consecrated to the Sacred Heart of Jesus. He became associated with the Franciscan Order and was especially pleased that he had been enrolled in the Association of the Perpetual Rosary.

At the age of fifteen, Aldo died in Naples on December 5, 1934. During the examination process for beatification, his body was entombed in the basilica of St. Dominico Maggiore in Naples. In 1958, 24 years after his death, the Vatican accepted his Cause for Beatification. ✝

Servant of God Alexia Gonzalez-Barros

1971 – 1985
14 years old
SPAIN

*S*he had favorite television programs and knew about video
games. She bought record albums, went shopping, and liked
nice clothes, movies, and sailing. She was a normal girl — yet, at the
same time, a teenager whose everyday holiness, heroism, and sanctity
in the face of an agonizing illness are now being recognized around
the world as deserving of beatification.

Alexia had the good fortune to be born into a loving and deeply
religious family. Her father, Francisco Gonzalez-Barros — "Paco"—
was a successful businessman in Madrid. Her mother Ramona —
"Moncha"— was a well-bred woman of deep spirituality. Both parents
instilled in their children a love of church and gave them an admirable
example of pious Christian living.

Their first child was Maria José. Next came five boys, the two
youngest dying in infancy. And then some years later — quite unexpectedly, but joyously, welcomed — came Alexia, born March 7, 1971.
During this pregnancy, as she no doubt did for the others as well,

Moncha prayed a special novena to Our Lady. After each of her Communions she would also pray, "Grant, O Lord, that this child participate in the grace of this Communion." This virtuous mother was not only the heart of the family, but also its religious guide.

We are told that the children knew that neither the "stork" nor any other creature brought the babies but the Child Jesus Himself, and it was He who also took them away. They were taught to love God and the Blessed Mother and participated in family devotions to St. Joseph and their Guardian Angel. They were encouraged to recite both the morning offering and special prayers in the evening. Frequent confession was recommended, and the liturgical seasons of Advent, Lent, and Easter were carefully observed.

Maria José, fifteen at the time of Alexia's birth, joined Opus Dei as a numerary member and left home to live in a center. She had been like a little mother to Alexia, so when she left, Alexia deeply felt the loss. But the boys in the family willingly kept her occupied. Alfredo, the eldest (and her godfather), spent hours playing games and doing crossword puzzles with her. Francisco, the artist of the family, taught her to draw and paint and even allowed her to use his oils and canvases. José Damian was her confidant who took her to movies and shopping and was her almost constant companion. Alexia was the darling of the family, but despite the attention, she was never spoiled. Indeed, her family often told her, "How could we have lived without you?"

Alexia began school at the age of four at the nearby Colegio de Jesus Maestro, conducted by the Company of St. Theresa of Jesus. Alexia's early school years were the happiest chapters in her short life. She loved her teachers and made many friends. Not all these friends were as loyal as she was, but she never held their activities against them and continued to invite them to her birthday parties. We are told that she never allowed anger to get the better of her. She was also a good sport in the face of defeat or failure and tried her best to hide her feelings, even when it was difficult for her to do so.

One example of her consideration for others was the time in school when her deskmate, an irritable and spoiled little girl, kept scratching Alexia's hands until they bled. When Moncha saw the condition of her daughter's hands, she decided to speak with the teacher, but Alexia pleaded with her not to, saying that she was afraid the girl would be punished. Instead, after several of these incidents, Alexia spoke to the girl herself; that seemed to stop the girl's behavior. (We are told that Alexia was not unhappy when the girl was later moved to another desk!)

Alexia was also a very generous child and helpful to everyone, particularly her schoolmates, to whom she lent a large number of pencils, erasers, and the like that were never returned. She was particularly sensitive to others' feelings. Once, on her way to school, she saw a young mother harshly scolding her daughter and slapping the child in the face. We are told that Alexia left for school earlier from then on in an effort not to witness a repeat of that wrenching scene.

Moncha helped prepare Alexia for her first confession when she was six years old and already devoutly reciting the family rosary. After confessing for the first time, Moncha noticed her daughter genuflecting very reverently, twice, before the tabernacle. When asked about it, Alexia responded, "I tell Him things, Mommy. I say, 'Jesus, may I always do what You want.'" Alexia made this offering each time she genuflected. At this tender age, she was already making frequent spiritual communions.

She made examinations of conscience with extreme care, even taking to writing her 'sins' in a notebook. Some of the notations read: "When my brothers tease me, I get upset. Its [sic] so hard to get up in the morning. Its [sic] so difficult to sit down and study. I complain a lot." Now and then she slipped in her resolutions, but she would always come back to her desire "to always do what the Lord wants me to do."

For the twenty-fifth anniversary of their marriage, Paco and Moncha decided on a celebration in Rome with the family; to all concerned, this also seemed an ideal time for Alexia to receive her first

Holy Communion. Alexia anticipated this with great happiness, because she had come to love Opus Dei and knew that its founder, the future St. Josemaria Escriva, was buried in the Eternal City.

And so it was that the family attended Holy Mass in the crypt, where Alexia received Our Lord by St. Escriva's tomb. Later Msgr. Alro del Portillo, St. Escriva's successor, asked her, "Alexia, do you realize that you are the first little girl to receive her first Holy Communion at the feet of our father (referring to St. Escriva)?"

She answered enthusiastically, "Yes, Father." Upon further questioning, she told the Monsignor, "Father, I pray a lot for you," adding that her confessor was an Opus Dei priest, "and he loves you too."

During their visit to Rome, the family was fortunate enough to attend a general audience with the pope in St. Peter's Square, and even had obtained invitations permitting them to get closer to the pope. As the pope descended to meet the people, Alexia suddenly darted away from her family. To their amazement, they saw a woman lift her over the barricade into the arms of a Swiss Guard, who allowed her to run to the pope with other children. She stood before him until it was her turn, then handed him a note she had written for him. The pope accepted it, touched her forehead in blessing, and then realized Alexia was trying to reach up to kiss him. So, to the continued amazement of her family, the pope obligingly bent over and kissed her on the forehead saying, "What an affectionate little girl you are!" (A picture of Alexia holding her note as she stood before the pope is printed in her biographies.)

Of course, Alexia was a normal little girl as well. When she was twelve, she confided to her mother that she had a crush on a certain young boy named Alphonsus, whom she saw at Palamos, where she often took sailing lessons. (She never met the boy, but two years later, when she knew she was dying, she made mention of him.)

That same year, an abortion law was being debated in parliament. This distressed her so much she wrote letters to the editors of several newspapers, and one was actually published by the Madrid paper, *YA*. It read, in part:

I am twelve years old and the seventh child. I thank God a lot for having sent me to a family who wanted me. If my mother were one of those who kill their children before they are born, I wouldn't be here today. Here's what I have to say to them: Please stop killing your children . . .

Alexia knew her religious and civic responsibilities very well. She encouraged her classmates to attend anti-abortion rallies and, at one rally, saw Mother Teresa of Calcutta. She again saw the pope when he visited Madrid in 1982; during the same year she and her family made a pilgrimage to Alba de Tormes to visit the shrine of St. Teresa of Ávila, to whom both she and the pope were particularly devoted.

But when she was thirteen, Alexia's life changed dramatically. Previously, she had always been a healthy young girl, but in the spring of 1984, she started to complain about back pains. She was brought to the doctor, who x-rayed the area but found nothing unusual. Early the next year, when the pain continued, she was again examined. This time, the pain was diagnosed as originating with muscle contractions, similar to a stiff neck. Another examination would have ended with a similar diagnosis if Alexia had not finally mentioned, "I can't move my hand."

After more X-rays, the doctor cautioned, "She must not move at all — the slightest motion could leave her paralyzed. Her spinal column is damaged." A biopsy of extracted tissue proved negative, to the family's great relief. But immediate surgery was called for to repair a break in her spinal column. This first operation lasted four hours, implanting a portion of her hipbone to secure the break. After more tests, she was put in a traction device that kept the spinal column extended to avoid pressure. It was an uncomfortable position that caused many a sleepless night. She endured many injections for every test — a particular trial for Alexia, as she never overcame her phobia of needles.

Despite the seriousness of the situation, however, Alexia did not shed a tear or express any fear, but joined the family in prayer in which they committed the future into God's hands. Clinging to her devotion to St. Josemaria Escriva, she expressed the desire to have his holy card placed where she could always see it from her hospital bed.

One month after checking into the hospital, Alexia celebrated her fourteenth birthday with all the nuns of the hospital around her bed singing to her and giving her as a gift, a poster that read: "God needs people like you!" She was convinced, as she told her mother, that it was the love of Jesus that moved everyone to be so kind to her.

Among the many kindnesses was that of a friend, Maria José Monterde, who loaned Alexia a rosary that once belonged to St. Escriva, saying, "Keep it until you get well." She often used this rosary after she said her night prayers, frequently kissing Escriva's relic.

But Alexia was not getting better. Her arms often cramped painfully; her legs were weak and gradually becoming paralyzed. Because of her deteriorating condition, more tests were performed in a different hospital by a different set of doctors. These tests included a scan that at last revealed the root cause of the paralysis and pain — a tumor in the cervical vertebrae, undetected earlier, now pressing on the spinal column. While comparing this new scan with the one taken before the first operation, doctors were dismayed to realize that the tumor had been there all along, but had been completely overlooked by the surgeon. A second operation was deemed necessary to remove the tumor. Although Alexia is said to have shed tears at the news, she bravely answered that she was "fine" when asked how she felt.

Alexia prepared herself for her second operation by confessing her faults, receiving Holy Communion, and praying quietly for over half an hour. She finished her prayers with, "Jesus, I want You to cure me. I want to get well. But if You don't want it that way, then I want what You want." In this, she offered her life to God with childlike simplicity.

The operation lasted three hours and revealed that the tumor was malignant — yet another unpleasant surprise for the family, after the first negative biopsy. But this was not the only shock they all had to endure: when Alexia mentioned that the incision made during the first operation was hurting — and because it had never healed — the doctor took the opportunity to open it and examine it carefully. To the horror of all concerned, he discovered that pieces of gauze had been left in the wound since the first operation.

To add to Alexia's troubles, in this second hospital, the doctors were excellent and kind, but the nurses were not. She was the brunt of their rudeness, sharp comments, rough handling, and insensitivity. In spite of this, she always responded in a friendly manner so that, in time, the nurses began to respond in like fashion. When Moncha noted, "People change when you deal with them affectionately," her daughter responded, "Yes, be friendly . . . and give them presents."

Eight days following the operation, the diagnosis was confirmed: Alexia had Ewing's sarcoma, an extremely grave but curable cancer that required radio therapy and another change of hospitals, this time to one that specialized in the treatment of cancer. While in this hospital, on being moved from a cart to an X-ray table, Alexia fell and hit her back on the edge of the table. Fortunately, her brother Francisco caught her before she hit the floor. One can only imagine the pain she suffered.

At this time the family wondered how to tell Alexia the seriousness of her condition, but they worried needlessly. She accepted the situation with a serenity that amazed everyone.

She was careful to hide her sufferings under a cloak of cheerfulness, in an effort not to cause anxiety to her parents and three brothers, but many difficulties arose from her treatment. A catheter clogged and had to be reinserted; another catheter had to be inserted into the jugular vein. Puncture wounds in her back — from the large needles used for her treatments — festered. Sores in her mouth and throat made it difficult for her to speak or eat; she battled dizziness, discomfort from the neck brace, and the effects of the endless stream of medications. One part of her treatment involved giving Alexia medication that made her overwhelmingly nauseous, with frequent vomiting. Yet, despite leg cramps, the head-to-shoulder brace, the nausea, and the vomiting, she repeatedly prayed, "Jesus, may I always do what You want." She lost her hair, and so much weight she appeared gaunt, but she met each challenge with patience and a pleasant word.

Of course, many people were praying for her, in addition to the fervent prayers offered by her family. From the beginning of her sickness, her daily prayer was: "Lord, for all who pray for me, return their prayers a hundredfold; for all those who do favors for me, pay them back a hundredfold as well." It could be accurately claimed that Alexia prayed almost constantly.

After a second round of treatments, Alexia was released from the hospital to stay at home for a few days. This last visit home ended on June 12, when she journeyed with her family to Pamplona and her fourth hospital, where another operation would be performed to determine the amount of radiation to be applied to her neck and insert a new device and catheter to enable the administration of medications without the need of injections.

Her room in this new hospital was bright and cheerful, with a crucifix and an image of the Blessed Virgin. And there was a chapel, which Alexia visited for a considerable length of time. After a number of tests, doctors deemed it necessary to correct the first grafting and destroy any residue from the tumor. On the morning of this operation, Alexia devoutly received Holy Communion, and then endured seventeen hours in the operating room. Following this third operation, the doctors told her family that it was necessary to place Alexia in a partial cast, and that they had installed a metallic crown around her head. This crown was held in place by four screws imbedded in her scalp. Although the contraption startled the family, Alexia accepted her condition calmly and seemed to improve. Her radiotherapy sessions made her look sunburned, but her appetite improved so that she was eating almost every hour, and the family was tremendously relieved.

But this increased appetite produced a new setback. Alexia gained so much weight that the cast became too small, and its edges began digging into her skin. She was also perspiring from the summer heat, and a long wound formed all around the edges of the cast. Her nurses remember how Alexia bore the discomfort without complaint, although she had difficulty breathing.

Finally, a fourth operation became necessary, which took eight hours. In the end, Alexia still had a cast and the metallic crown. Some new surgical wounds at the back of her neck and on her hip refused to heal; she had to bear this in addition to oppressive heat, potent medications, immobility, tedious treatments, and chemotherapy. This condition lasted two weeks until doctors at last found a medication effective in healing the wounds. The other discomforts remained, and her condition seemed martyrdom in itself; yet she continued to face it with patience and not a word of complaint.

Alexia was allowed to return to the apartment the family had rented in Pamplona, although this presented other problems: it was difficult to place her in a wheelchair and get her in and out of a taxi for a daily return to the hospital for therapy. But soon she was unable to do even that much. Her condition worsened, with the onset of headaches that became unbearable. It was then that she began talking about heaven and asking those around her to describe heaven for her. One day she said to her mother, "You know, Mom, I already want to go to heaven."

The headaches became particularly acute toward the end of November, but she refused medications because they gave only temporary relief. Tests to determine the cause of the headaches revealed a metastasis in the meninges, a hopeless condition. Francisco, Alexia's brother, remembered that another Spanish girl, Montserrat Grases — seventeen years old and a member of Opus Dei — had also died of Ewing's sarcoma. (Her biography is given in this book.) In spite of this latest downturn, mother and daughter prayed the devotion of The Three Hail Marys, in addition to other prayers, each night.

Alexia's condition was now so serious that her brothers and sister were summoned to the hospital immediately. Moncha placed a scapular of Our Lady of Mount Carmel around her daughter's neck and placed in her hands the rosary that belonged to St. Josemaria. Alexia was now breathing heavily and seemed to be in agony. Moncha asked if she wanted to go to confession; Alexia quickly agreed. The hospital chaplain heard her confession, gave her Holy Communion, and administered both the sacrament of Confirmation and the Sacrament of the Sick, which she received with keen attention and recollection. Afterward, she thanked the good priest and became absorbed in deep contemplation. When a nurse came to administer a medication, she pleaded, "Please, not now. I want to be alone with Jesus."

During the following few days, Alexia made frequent spiritual communions. Because she had difficulty swallowing, she was permitted to receive only a small piece of the Blessed Sacrament. She was perfectly aware that Jesus was coming soon to claim her, and she impatiently awaited Him. In her hand was a list she had dictated to her mother — a list of names that she wanted to pray for when she reached heaven. It seems that many of her visitors, including her nurses and doctors, had asked her prayers for certain individuals, and these were dutifully included in her list. Some of those mentioned:

"For Opus Dei and the Father.
"For all those who pray for me.
"For the boyfriend of the nurse in the x-ray room.
"For all the children in the ward that they be well.
"For all those who have done me a favor from the time I got sick..."

The list concluded with her usual prayer, "Sweet Heart of Mary, be my salvation. Jesus, Joseph, Mary, I give you my heart and my soul. Sacred Heart of Jesus, I trust in You. Hail, Most Pure Mary."

Alexia's serenity impressed everyone who saw her at this time. Her doctor, the Chief of Pediatrics, called her room "the anteroom to heaven." One of the nurses, a non-practicing Catholic, exclaimed, "I can't enter that room. How can one die with so much joy?" And a priest who often visited announced, "When someone would ask me what I saw in Alexia, the only thing that comes to my mind is this: sanctity."

Oxygen now relieved her difficulty in breathing, although all signs indicated she was blind. But she "saw" in a supernatural way: at various times, she said that evil spirits were encircling her bed. At this, the family promptly doused her bed with holy water.

And then there was her angel, whom she had long ago named Hugo. At times she was aware of him beside her, then would claim he'd left. But she was undaunted. "I know," she said, "we'll go to heaven together, and when we get there, I wouldn't mind if he wanted to be with the other angels."

While Moncha was telling her saintly daughter that the Blessed Virgin loved her very much, she asked, "Alexia, do you love Jesus?" The answer was a prompt and firm, "Yes."

Moncha then asked, "And are you happy?"

Alexia answered, "Yes!" and breathed her last. It was 11:05 a.m., December 5, 1985.

Upon her death, Alexia's face became rosy and assumed an unearthly beauty and serenity. But as the body was being prepared for burial, bruises were discovered all over her back, as though she had received a cruel beating. Ghastly wounds were revealed: the scars on her neck, the screws in her head, and countless needle marks from injections — wounds, to many, almost reminiscent of a crucifixion.

The entire medical staff came to pay their last respects and declared to the mother, "She is a child-saint." Many others said, "We envy you for having such a saintly daughter." One of the doctors went so far as to assure an aunt, "We shall see your niece honored on the altars of the church."

Afterward, her family returned the rosary of St. Josemaria; the scapular was given to Dr. Chamorro, as Moncha thought Alexia would have wanted it that way.

It is amazing to note that a book written by Sr. Maria Victoria Molins, *Alexia: A Teenager's Experience of Love and Pain,* was published only six months after Alexia's death. Her story was published in pamphlet form and distributed throughout the world, from the United States to Latin America, Canada, Europe, Asia, Australia, and Africa. Letters to the family for more information came "in droves." Magazines quickly published her story, and a radio station in Madrid aired a fifteen-part series about her. When prayer cards were printed, the first 15,000 were depleted in just five days.

Alexia's courage in the face of her suffering as she lived out her prayer — "May I always do what You want"— has been an inspiration to countless souls around the world. To the great satisfaction of those who knew her, documents are now being prepared for the introduction of her Cause for Beatification. ✝

Servant of God Anfrosina Berardi

1920 – 1933
13 years old
ITALY

*A*nfrosina Berardi was born on December 6, 1920, at S. Marco di Preturo, Italy, the last of nine children born into a modest farming family. From childhood she was known for her gentle nature and her practice of virtue, especially her acceptance of the childish troubles common between the siblings of a large family. Her love of God and the Blessed Virgin were extraordinary and recognized by all who knew her.

When she was eleven years old, in April 1931, she was stricken by a sudden attack of appendicitis. When the condition did not improve, she was taken to the hospital at Aquila. Four days later she underwent an operation, but the procedure did not totally remove the infection; it continued to spread, with pain that intensified into spasmodic cramps. Her heroic acceptance of this acute pain produced the extraordinary virtue that became known throughout the area.

On her bed of pain, she prayed and accepted her condition without complaint. Many from nearby areas who heard of her virtues were irresistibly attracted to the sense of the supernatural and paid visits to her bedside. This inspired many to a life of prayer, and others to reform their lives. Others petitioned her to pray for their intentions. The visitors to her bedside were numerous and, in spite of her pain, she greeted everyone with a smile and a word of welcome. She answered many questions and promised to pray for many of her visitors.

When Anfrosina saw that her mother was especially worried about her condition, she reminded her that the Blessed Virgin was looking after her. When she knew death was near, she cautioned her mother not to cry because it would be a happy event . . . because she was going to meet the Madonna.

After two years of acute suffering, the thirteen-year-old child died piously on March 13, 1933. She was buried in the parish church of St. Mark at Preturo, the city of her birth, in the church where she had often received the sacraments.

In 1962, the Archbishop of Aquila began the informative process for her Cause for Beatification. The last important action taken on her case was made in 1993. ✝

Servant of God Angela Iacobellis

1948 – 1961
13 years old
ITALY

*A*ngela had the privilege of being baptized in the Basilica of St. Peter in Rome with the names of Angela, Maria, Teresa, and Ida. Because of the place where she became a child of the Catholic Church, she developed a great love of the pope. She also had an immense love for Jesus and Mary, as well as a lifelong devotion to St. Michael the Archangel.

Although Angela was born in Rome on October 16, 1948, she spent a large part of her life in Naples because of the difficult postwar time when her family's economic situation made it necessary to relocate.

Even at a very tender age, Angela was distressed at seeing the suffering of others, so much so that she gave away many of her toys to poor children. After her first Holy Communion, her devotion to the Eucharist compelled her to stop for a visit each time she passed a church, and no one could go to bed at night without having recited the Rosary. She had a horror of sin so deep that, when she heard improper language, she recited the *Regina Coeli*.

During the summer, the family began the practice of journeying to Assisi for a few days. For Angela, the Basilica of Saint Clare held the greatest attraction. It was her pleasure to help the sisters, especially in encouraging visiting women to cover themselves more modestly before entering the sacred places. She was attracted to the Franciscan spirituality and once mentioned that she would like to be buried in the Church of Saint Clare in Naples.

Angela had many talents. She was a good student, often assigned to help others with their schoolwork. Indeed, she frequently missed the chance to take an afternoon walk with her mother, something she enjoyed immensely, so that she could visit the home of a student who needed help. She loved music, dancing, and — above all — sketching. She even made amusing caricatures of people she loved.

Then one day Angela, who had always enjoyed good health , suddenly lost her appetite and became very pale. Her mother took her to the doctor, who ordered a test that required a puncture of the sternum, a very painful procedure that she tolerated with great resignation. Not until she was on a pilgrimage to Lourdes did Angela know the results of the test: she had leukemia.

Angela's relatives made pilgrimages, novenas were recited, and heaven was besieged for a miracle. Angela knew very well that it would take a miracle to restore her to health, but seeing so many efforts made for her recovery, she one day told her mother not to worry; she had asked the help of the Madonna of the Rosary in Pompeii.

Angela and her mother returned briefly to Rome to consult another doctor and, while there, visited some of Angela's favorite churches. In a display of emotion, Angela caressed many of the statues, apparently knowing that this would be her last time in the Eternal City.

She returned briefly to school but then had to quit altogether when she experienced a hemorrhage from the nose. Blood transfusions were ordered and, later, when she mentioned the pain in her back, more transfusions were administered. Her twelfth birthday was a very quiet one, and the next Christmas was not very happy for the family; Angela could not wear her new clothes, as she was then confined to bed, nor was she interested in her presents. Her only comfort came from a rosary she had carefully placed under her pillow, and from holding close to her heart the relics of St. Térèsa and Pope St. Pius X. She accepted her situation and her impending death as the will of God and without complaint, much to the edification of all who visited her.

The doctor came the morning of March 27, 1961, to prescribe medicines and to order the use of oxygen to help her breathe. But as soon as he left, Angela experienced a respiratory crisis; she died with such a pleasant expression on her face that relatives at first didn't suspect she was actually dead.

Because she had requested it, this little girl was buried in the Church of St. Clare in Naples. In 1997, however — with grand ceremony — Angela's body was disinterred for the canonical recognition required for the Cause for Beatification; examiners were amazed to find that, after 36 years, the little body had not suffered corruption. It was entombed in a chapel dedicated to her in the Church of S. Giovanni dei Fiorentini on November 21, 1997.

Devotion to the little thirteen-year-old has spread beyond Italy, with many reporting cures, conversions, and assistance of various kinds. The last action on Angela's Cause for Beatification was made in 1997. ✝

Servant of God Angelina Pirini

1922 – 1940
18 years old
ITALY

*A*ngelina is perhaps the only teenager mentioned in this volume who fell into ecstasies after Holy Communion. This took place during the last years of her life, although her early life gave no indication of the high degree of sanctity she would reach before her death.

She was a normal child born at Celle di Sala, near the community of Cesenatico in northeastern Italy, to Luigi and Dina Pirini. She received the sacraments in due course and attended school, where she was distinguished by a quick intelligence, but she remained only until the fifth grade. After that, she was apprenticed to a tailor. From then on, if not at work, she was at home, helping her mother with all the ordinary duties of housekeeping, which she performed responsibly and generously.

She was inclined to all things religious, but 1934 in particular was a decisive year in her spirituality. She was twelve years old that year when she felt the need to assist every day at Holy Mass. She communicated with great reverence, staying afterward for a long time in thanksgiving. Her love of the Holy Eucharistic was extraordinary, and it was from this devotion that she progressed into a deep relationship with the Eucharistic Lord and advanced to a high degree of perfection. She once wrote: "Oh Jesus. You are my only love — my thoughts are always fixed on You." Another time she wrote: "I feel that the divine love has completely invaded my spirit and I feel myself burn from this inextinguishable flame."

Her deep love of God and desire to help others prompted her to enroll in Catholic Action and participate in the charitable activities of her parish whenever her duties permitted. She eventually became an officer in the parochial division of the Catholic Action group and distinguished herself for her ardent zeal and her tireless work, earning the respect of everyone with her kind, charitable, most patient, and good attitude toward all.

When Fr. Joseph Marchi arrived in the parish, he soon became her spiritual director and guided her for six years. It was he who gave her permission to make a temporary vow of virginity in 1937, when she was fifteen years old. She would be permitted to make a perpetual vow of virginity a year later.

But before making this permanent vow, Angelina — who had always previously enjoyed good health — was stricken with appendicitis. Surgery, medication, and therapy followed, but even with all that, she was brought almost to death. After a second operation, a new diagnosis was made: incurable intestinal tuberculosis.

Despite this ailment and its intense suffering, though, Angelina almost seemed pleased with her condition, as it would enable her to participate in the sufferings of Our Lord. She wanted also to apply the pain to make reparation for her imperfections and the sins of the world, as well as the sanctification of souls, particularly those of priests. She accepted everything with great serenity and joy, edifying all who came in contact with her.

On June 16, 1938, the feast of Corpus Christi, Angelina consecrated herself in a special way to the holy will of God. She asked nothing for herself, but only for holy souls who would love God, and especially for missionaries who would be zealous in their apostolic works.

After receiving the last sacraments and the Holy Eucharist, she died on October 2, 1940, at the age of eighteen. She was first buried in the cemetery adjacent to the parish church, but so many townspeople and others were visiting the site, with many reporting favors received in response to her intercessory prayers, that the diocese began an investigation.

The canonical recognition of the remains was made on October 12, 1985. Afterward, the remains of this teenager were taken in a solemn procession into the parish church where they were entombed in a magnificent marble urn. In this small chapel, situated above the tomb, is a large picture of St. Maria Goretti — who, like Angelina, greatly valued the virtue of purity.

We learn of Angelina's intense spiritual life, and her love of God and the Blessed Virgin, from her diary, which includes sections titled "Spiritual Accounts" and "The Spiritual Will." In this document, she wrote extensively on her love of the Holy Eucharist; from these writings we learn the height she attained in the spiritual life.

The last action taken on her Cause for Beatification was made in 1992. ✝

Servant of God Angiolino Bonetta

1948 – 1963
15 years old
ITALY

hrough the years, the Church has given us many saintly young-sters as models of virtue, such as Sts. Dominic Savio and Maria Goretti (along with those mentioned in this book). One who deserves attention for his heroic acceptance of suffering is Angiolino Bonetta, who died at the tender age of fifteen.

He was born on September 18, 1948, into a pious and hardworking family. His father, Francis, was an agricultural day laborer in Cigole, near Brescia, in northern Italy, until he turned to a more lucrative position as a truck driver. His mother, Julia Scaratti, was a cloth repairer employed by Marzotto Manerbio. While both his parents were at work, Angiolino's older sister Maria cared for him. From all accounts, Angiolino was a good child, of a vivacious nature and always cheerful.

He attended the primary grades in Brescia "with great profit," and was known by his many friends as being athletic, affectionate, and spontaneous. Often, he was also the instigator of little tricks played on teachers and fellow students. A "born actor," he enjoyed performing in happy interpretations and in funny sketches. His teachers remember him as being good, generous with everyone, and full of energy.

For all his playfulness and mischief making, however, Angiolino could also be very serious. He received his First Holy Communion at the age of seven, in what he considered to be a great celebration. From then on, he received Holy Communion every day and quickly advanced in virtue.

After the completion of his primary studies, he entered the institute Artigianelli (Piamarta) in Brescia, where he was prepared to study for a professional position in the manufacturing world in Brescia. In this school, conducted by the Congregation of the Holy Family of Nazareth, the boy flourished scholastically and athletically, participating in races, football, and other athletic endeavors. Not long after he was settled happily in the school, however, he began to suffer pain in his right knee. The knee developed swelling, but this was blamed on his activities and occasional falls, so the swelling was ignored for a long time. When he lost weight and began limping, the condition could no longer be ignored. His mother took him to the hospital for radiological examinations, which eventually revealed bone cancer. Angiolino was then twelve years old. It was the beginning of his Calvary, but, touched by grace, he totally abandoned himself to the will of God.

Angiolino returned to his family confident that the chemotherapy treatments would have a positive effect; but, when his condition went from relative comfort to severe pain, he returned to the hospital. Doctors eventually had to amputate his leg on January 22, 1963. What others considered a great tragedy, Angiolino accepted as a gift, realizing that he could spiritually benefit from the ordeal. To a nun who suggested to him that he offer his sufferings for souls, he responded, "I have already offered all to Jesus for the conversion of sinners. I am not afraid, Jesus always comes to help me."

During his hospital stay, he encouraged other suffering patients and obtained several conversions. He left an indelible impression on many with his kind words and inspired many to a life of prayer. Best of all, he maintained his keen sense of humor, surprising visitors who expected a solemn-faced little victim. All were amazed that he had a quick smile for everyone and radiated joy and hope.

Unfortunately the cancer metastasized, causing Angiolino increased pain. Necessary medical procedures added to that distress, but Angiolino is said to have prayed to his beloved Madonna and was daily supported by his reception of the Holy Eucharist. The nursing nuns were edified by his willing acceptance of pain for the sake of souls and began to recommend to him certain patients in difficult physical and mental states. One such patient was a Swiss Protestant. For the well being of this man, Angiolino spent a whole night in prayer reciting the Holy Rosary, his favorite devotion.

Not long after the amputation, he met the (future) Servant of God Msgr. Luigi Novarese, who had been miraculously cured of tuberculosis of the bone. After his cure, Msgr. Novarese founded two organizations: Volunteers to Help Alleviate Suffering and the Silent Laborers of the Cross. Msgr. Novarese frequently visited Angiolino, counseling him on the value of suffering and the acceptance of pain, which united him closely to Our Lord. Angiolino had already been accepting his situation with peace and joy. So, encouraged by the Monsignor, he decided to join the Silent Laborers of the Cross.

He entered the hospice of the founder, Cuore Immacolato di Maria di Re, on September 21, 1962. For the ceremony of his profession, he was carried on a stretcher to the chapel, where he was placed before a statue of the Madonna. Raising his arms to his heavenly mother, he pronounced private vows of poverty, chastity, and obedience, and with a smile added: "O Immaculate Heart of Mary, you are my refuge." Witnesses to the little ceremony were Msgr. Alfonso Carinci, Msgr. Luigi Corti, and members of the community. All were edified by the pale Angiolino, who held his lighted candle steadily in one hand while joining in the singing of *Ave Maris Stella*. As a member of the community, he was to say that suffering was his vocation.

From time to time, when he was stronger in body and spirit, he would return home for visits with his family. They would take him to the parish church of St. Martin in a wheelchair, where townspeople and friends greeted him. But overall, he continued to grow progressively weaker and consumed with pain. His only comfort was in holding a crucifix and a relic of St. Bernadette given to him by Msgr. Novarese. He had also been given a little grey stone taken from the cave of Massabielle (where Our Lady appeared at Lourdes).

His family has kept this and other devotional objects, together with a statue of Our Lady and his rosary, in his room. Another great comfort are the many photographs of Angiolino taken during this time, always showing a broadly smiling youngster holding his beloved rosary.

He was particularly devoted to the Madonna of Lourdes and turned to her as to his true mother. Many times he was absorbed in silent contemplative prayer with closed eyes and a serene expression. The day before he died he told his mother, "I have made a pact with the Madonna. When the hour arrives, she will come to take me. I have asked her to permit me to make my purgatory on this earth, not in the other world. When I die I will immediately fly to heaven." On January 27, 1963, in the presence of his family, various priests, and medical personnel, he was administered the Sacrament of the Sick.

The death of the young boy, in the early morning hours of January 28, 1963, was truly edifying. He laboriously opened his eyes, looked intently at his mother and the bystanders, and held tightly in his hand a crucifix and the relic of Saint Bernadette. He fixed a long gaze toward the statue of the Madonna and fell asleep in the arms of his heavenly Mother.

News of his death quickly flashed to Cigole and Brescia. Many recounted with great emotion the various occasions when they had talked with him and how affected they were by having known him. Everywhere were whispers, "He was a little saint!"

So many mourners attended his funeral that diocesan officials took notice. Realizing that he had reached "breathtaking heights of Christian heroism," they opened his Cause for Beatification in 1998 and awarded him the title Servant of God. During the ceremony that introduced the Cause, his mother and family were present, as well as members of the Silent Laborers of the Cross, members of the parishes of Cigole and Brescia, and a large number of clergymen. Also present was Angiolino's spiritual director, Msgr. Luigi Novarese (now also awaiting beatification). ✝

St. Anna Wang

1886 – 1900
14 years old
CHINA

*D*uring the Boxer Rebellion of 1900, with its drive to rid China of Westerners and Chinese Christians, a large number of Catholics were arrested and martyred for the faith. Among them was fourteen-year-old Anna Wang, the child of Christian parents.

Documented testimonies used in the canonization process reveal that Anna was born in Majiazhuang and was only five years old when her mother died. Six years later, she was promised in marriage, but she stood firm and rejected the plans made in her name.

When the Boxers arrived in Majiazhuang on July 21, 1900, they captured a group of Christians and gave them an ultimatum: "The government has banned the practice of Western religions. If you renounce your religion, you will be set free; if you refuse, we will kill you."

Once again, Anna's strong character exerted itself, and she steadfastly refused to recant, even though her stepmother had renounced the faith and urged Anna to do the same. Anna was known to have stated, "I believe in God. I am a Christian. I do not renounce God. Jesus, save me!"

The next night, Anna and a group of friends prayed until dawn. The Boxers made good on their threat quickly, leading the Christians to their execution the next morning.

The courage of the condemned was outstanding. When a nine-year-old boy, Andre Wang Tianqing, was to be executed, many non-Christian witnesses tried to save him. But his mother cried out, "I am a Christian; my son is a Christian. You will have to kill us both." The Boxers were pleased to oblige. After little Andre knelt down, he smiled at his mother as the executioner lowered an ax to his head. In addition to this child and his mother, five other mothers with their children were killed, including a ten-month-old baby who was grabbed by the leg, cut in half, and thrown on the body of his dead mother.

After witnessing the killing of little Andre, Anna knelt in fervent prayer. With one of the Boxers standing over her, she was once more given the option of being set free if she denied the faith. Again she refused, saying, "I prefer to die rather than give up my faith."

Angered by her firm statement, the soldier cut off her right arm and asked her again, "Do you deny your religion?" Anna remained silent. Enraged still more at her refusal, he struck her again. It was then that she was heard to say, "The door of heaven is open." After whispering the name of Jesus three times, she lowered her head and was promptly decapitated.

Over the objections of the Chinese government, Pope John Paul II canonized 120 Christians on October 1, 2000. These included the martyrs of the Boxer Rebellion, as well as martyred missionaries from five European countries, who died in China between 1648 and 1930. Of all the martyrs canonized that day, the one who has gained the most attention is brave little Anna Wang, who affirmed her beliefs and heroically faced death at only fourteen years of age. +

Venerable Anne de Guigne

1911 – 1922
11 years old
FRANCE

We read in the lives of many saints that their infancy or earliest childhood was distinguished by definite indications of future sanctity, but this could not be said of Anne de Guigne. She displayed a tempestuous spirit, a determination to have her own way even among older playmates, an inclination to be bossy with her younger brother and two sisters, and a deep jealousy when her mother showed attention to her little brother, who had succeeded her in the cradle. One biographer goes so far as to declare Anne a "tyrant."

Anne was a child of privilege, having for her father Jacques, Count de Guigne, who engaged in many charitable activities of the district; and for her mother Antoinette de Charette, a lady of culture. In the stately Chateau de la Cour, overlooking the lake of Annecy, the parents first welcomed Anne. Next came little Jacque, sometimes called JoJo; a sister, Madeleine, called Leleine; and Marie Antoinette, whose name was abbreviated to Marinette. Free from want and enjoying all that their position in life provided, theirs was a happy home, except when Anne displayed her temper!

At the first indication that France might be engaged in war, Jacques de Guigne rejoined his old regiment and was wounded. As he recuperated at home, little Anne assumed the task of caring for her father when her mother or the nurses weren't around him — bringing him books, fetching what he wanted, and playing nurse. The second time he was wounded, he was placed in a hospital, where Madame de Guigne and Anne visited him. This experience of seeing so many poor

44

men in rows of beds, suffering for their country, made a great impression on Anne.

The father's third wounding was his last. When news reached the family that he had died, Madame de Guigne was overwhelmed with grief. Having already been deeply impressed by seeing the sick men in the hospital, and watching her mother suffer from her loss, little almost-five-year-old Anne was changed forever. She realized that happiness in this life is fleeting and that sorrows and sufferings are frequent visitors, and thus decided that heaven and its happiness were the ultimate destiny of the good and virtuous.

She knew that to reach heaven, one must be good, so she determined that the way for her to be good was to obey her mother and to be kind to those with whom she came in contact. Following her father's death, Anne, being the oldest, did all she could to keep the others quiet so that their mother could rest, and she performed little services for her mother to relieve her grief.

When the new governess arrived in 1916, she was astonished to learn that Anne, now so sweet and gentle, had been a very troublesome child only a few months earlier. The governess once wrote:

> I was really charmed by the easy grace of her manner.... One could not help loving her. Although so tiny, there was something about her even then that inspired respect. She was very sensible too, and she had such a kind little heart.... Almost as soon as I arrived she took me around the garden and wanted me to pick some flowers saying, "Pick all the flowers you like and send them to your mother to comfort her." The next morning I heard a soft little knock at my door. It was the dear child coming to see if I had slept well....

Almost a year earlier, Anne had begun speaking about her first Holy Communion, even though she was not quite the age for its reception. Nevertheless, she was enrolled in Catechism class. Her teacher, Mother St. Raymond, wrote of her:

I soon saw that Anne was a very gifted child; but what struck me most was this: the others were never jealous of her, though she was cleverer than any of them and the youngest.... Every one of them loved and admired her. I think it was because she never tried to 'show off' or get the better of anyone.... she was as nice with some rather spoiled children as with those who behaved well. I do not think I ever saw her in a bad humor or upset over anything... she never even teased the other children, and this must have meant considerable self-control, for she was naturally so quick and sharp.

Although she had difficulty memorizing lessons, she nevertheless could explain in astonishingly clear and precise words the meaning of each lesson. When Mother St. Raymond asked permission from the bishop for Anne's reception of the Sacrament at such an early age, the bishop assigned the superior of the Jesuits to question her readiness. At first the priest scoffed that this tiny girl was ready, and asked her many questions in words different from those in the Catechism. Anne explained them all, much to the surprise of the holy priest. When he was satisfied that Anne was fully prepared, he left the room, remarking to Mother St. Raymond, "I wish you and I were as well prepared to receive Our Lord as this little girl is."

At the First Communion retreat, Anne took for her motto, "Obedience is the sanctity of children." After the reception of the sacrament, Anne was heard to say, "O, now I am quite, quite happy... from now on I will give my sacrifices to Mary so that she may give them to Jesus." When asked what she said to Jesus during prayer, Anne replied simply, "I tell Him I love Him."

Those who had seen Anne receive Holy Communion will never forget what they saw. One person commented, "She looked like a living monstrance. Her face was radiant." Even at her tender age, she was inspired to write simple little poems and canticles to be recited at the time of Holy Communion. As for her reception of the sacrament of Penance, a woman once asked the priest the identity of the little girl who had just left the confessional. When the priest asked why she wanted to know, she replied, "Why, Father, because she looked positively transfigured when she came out."

Even her governess reflected on her nature, "I have never known Anne to refuse a sacrifice." Only a few times did she show hesitation over an act of obedience or sacrifice, though sometimes there would be a little sign of the hard struggle she endured.

During a bout of influenza, when mustard poultices had to be applied to her chest, she endured the unpleasant process without complaint, saying all the time, "Jesus, I offer it to You."

When she became ill with paratyphoid, she was required to stay in bed for months. The usual fare given a patient during this time was mild, bland soup. Anne showed her love for God, and willingness to sacrifice herself, by eating all given her without complaint.

As she grew older, she not only looked after the others but also endeavored to please them by giving them her desserts and sweets. In fact, she so successfully hid her likes and dislikes that the elders completely forgot that she had any. If the other children wanted to play games she did not like, she participated nonetheless. If they wanted one of her toys — a certain little wheelbarrow, for example — she gladly relinquished it, saying, "It's all right. I don't mind if they want it." She met every opportunity for self-denial quickly and with a smile, and once was heard to say, "*Yes* is the nicest word we can say to Jesus."

Anne once learned that a fire in the village had destroyed the house of a poor widow with four small children. Distressed, she devised a method to help: she and the other children would have a bazaar. Of course, Anne could have asked her mother for money, but the children wanted to do this on their own. They saved their desserts and sweets, and collected various berries and nuts from the woods. All were carefully arranged in decorated stalls. They gathered flowers from the garden and put them out for sale, plus handcrafted articles, including tiny cradles scooped out of acorns, baskets carved from horse chestnuts, bags woven with rushes, and other little treasures. People from the village attended, and a sizable amount of money was collected by this eight-year-old, then presented happily to the poor widow.

Surrounded by comfort and wealth, Anne, remarkably, had a great respect and concern for the poor. Once she asked her mother how the poor kept warm in the winter. When she was told that many did not keep warm, Anne was troubled, so her mother suggested that she learn to knit and make some warm clothes for them. Anne began at once to learn simple knitting and made scarves and other little things for the poor.

Anne then began the custom of praying for sinners and would ask the nuns at school for someone who needed prayers. She was never happy unless she had some special soul to pray for.

When Anne was ten years old, she made these resolutions after attending a retreat.

> My soul is meant for Heaven. We take a lot of trouble over dressing our bodies, but think less about our souls. . . . There ought to be: First, cleanness (of soul), which means avoiding sin. Second, proper clothing, that is, doing our duty. Third, adornment, which means the good actions that we do of our own free will. . . . It depends on me. Mother cannot do the work for me.

She also wrote, "These are my faults: I am inclined to be proud and to be lazy, so a daily struggle is necessary for me." The child was determined to advance in the way of perfection.

It would seem that Anne had a presentiment of her own death when she neared her eleventh birthday. She began speaking of heaven as though it were a place she would soon visit and seemed eager for the day when she would be there. Years earlier, she had told her mother that during prayer, "I tell Jesus that I love Him, and then I talk about you and I ask Him to make the others good. I ask Him lots of things, and I pray for my sinners too . . . and I tell Him that I want to see Him." When Mother St. Joseph, the natural sister of Madame de Guigne, was asked to teach Anne how to pray, she commented, "What good should I do? I should only spoil her simplicity. God teaches that child." And God would soon be calling her to Himself.

Although Anne, for the most part, was a healthy child, she endured two painful illnesses and was subject to severe headaches. After enduring one of these headaches, Anne commented, "We have lots of joys here on earth, but they do not last; the only joy that lasts is to have made a sacrifice."

When she betrayed being in pain at school with a look of discomfort, Mother St. Raymond obeyed the doctor's orders by asking Anne to lie flat on a board; she did so without hesitation. Mother St. Raymond later recorded, "I often wondered at her patience. Very few children would have lain like that on a board without a word of complaint, and for such a long time. Her will ruled all her actions so that there was perfect order in her life. It was very striking to see such a brave will in such a frail little body."

As Anne was going down to dinner one evening, the pain in her head became so severe the poor child had to resort to her bed. Three days later, when the doctor arrived, her mother thought Anne was sleeping, but the doctor recognized that the little girl was in a coma. The diagnosis was meningitis. A while later she was conscious, but her face betrayed her agony so that it was painful to look at her.

When asked if she wanted to receive Holy Communion by a visiting priest, she said, "Yes" with such enthusiasm that the priest wrote later, "Never shall I forget that word. The whole desire of her soul was in it." Two days later, she received the Sacrament of the Sick, fully understanding what it was. Then her chest muscles became paralyzed, producing painful attacks of suffocation lasting hours at a time; Anne bore these struggles with admirable patience.

Once after a terrible crisis, Madame de Guigne whispered to her daughter, "You have been brave, darling. This will comfort the Heart of Our Lord and win over some of your sinners."

Anne gasped for joy. "Oh, Mother, I'm so glad. If it does that, I will bear lots more."

She lingered in torment without a word of complaint, although her face was often contorted with pain. Once, however, after a brief respite, Anne had a visit from one of the sisters. The nun left her room in tears, saying, "I thank God for having allowed me to see that child. She is indeed a saint. Her face looks simply angelic."

Anne's "birthday in heaven" was January 14, 1922. She gazed at a picture of the Blessed Mother and repeated word for word the *Hail Holy Queen*. Then, after looking at her earthly mother for the last time, she expired.

A few days later, her body was taken to Annecy-le-Vieux and interred in the family vault. When many cures and favors were attributed to the little victim of love, the bishop of Annecy, Msgr. Du Bois de la Villerabel, opened the canonical investigation into Anne's life and virtues in 1932. An exhumation of her remains then took place with the bishop, doctors, priests, Anne's mother, and other relatives in attendance. When the casket was opened, onlookers saw that the body was perfectly preserved. Those who had known Anne found her features exactly as they had been in life. Later, more than 300 people passed by the casket after waiting in cold rain and icy winds for the opportunity.

Pope John Paul II approved a decree on March 3, 1990, recognizing the heroic virtues of this eleven-year-old child by awarding her the title of Venerable. Little Anne now awaits beatification and canonization. ✝

Annie Zelikova

1924 – 1941
17 years old
CZECHOSLOVAKIA

The life of St. Thérèse of Lisieux and that of Annie Zelikova parallel each other in many respects: during their early years, both had an active spiritual life and were attracted to the Discalced Carmelite Order. Thérèse entered the cloister; Annie became a Carmelite tertiary. Both surrendered themselves to God's merciful love with their penances being offered for priests. Both made private sacrifices, concealed with a heavenly smile; in fact, Annie had what was called her "apostolate of the smile." Both corresponded a great deal, writing letters that are spiritual gems. Both died of tuberculosis at a young age, Thérèse being 24, Annie only 17; and finally, the last words of each are very similar. There are still many other instances in the life of Annie that recall similar expressions of love, resembling those of her spiritual counterpart.

But with all these similarities, there is one great difference in the two: their family backgrounds. Thérèse was born into an upper-middle-class family; Annie was a simple farm girl born in Moravia, in the central province of what was formerly known as Czechoslovakia. We can safely assert that Annie received many of her inspirations from the *Autobiography* of St. Thérèse, one of her favorite books. She also enjoyed other spiritual books: Fr. Graf's *Yes, Father* and Fr. Wickel, S.J.'s *Ecce Jesus*.

What we know of Annie comes largely from her own writings, including her record of spiritual exercises, retreats, and the letters she wrote as an apostolate. After Communism's demise — when spiritual literature was once again allowed — other biographies followed, demonstrating that this holy farm girl's story was not forgotten during the long religious suppression. Only after the dissolution of the Communist regime was it possible to initiate the process of beatification.

Annie was born on July 19, 1924, the first child of the family headed by Alois Zelikova. A second daughter followed three years later. Their father studied carpentry but was, in fact, a small farmer. Annie's religious upbringing was described as being solidly Catholic with images of the Blessed Virgin, protectress of the Moravian people, being displayed in every home and in innumerable shrines. Even today, the Moravian people perceive the Blessed Mother as being a living presence among her people.

Annie was not a paragon of virtue from the cradle, but was sometimes headstrong and often insisted on having her own way and being in charge. After her death, her spiritual advisor returned to Annie's home to find additional information for a book he was writing about her, and remarked to her relatives that Annie couldn't have been all that perfect from childhood, as it would seem. "She must have had some faults," he insisted.

Her younger sister replied that she did have a few faults, but "Just until her first Holy Communion, not after that."

It became Annie's practice to make Holy Mass the highlight of every day. One day when the two girls did not have school, their father expected them to help in the fields. Because his land was located a good distance from the town, their walk to it would have to begin early, and this would interfere with Annie's participation in the morning

Mass. Annie pleaded with her parents, promising that she would run very fast to catch up to them after Mass, and work extra hard to accomplish the work expected of her. Her parents relented.

Annie attended a school conducted by the Sisters of the Holy Cross, whose convent and school were very close to the Zelikova's home. These nuns, especially Sr. Ludmilla, knew exactly how to encourage and advise her spiritually.

When Annie was ten years old, she was permitted to join the sisters for a three-day retreat. Since the Christmas season was fast approaching, she was to write later:

I wanted a manger with many flowers of love as possible. . . . Up to now I loved Jesus, but now my desire grew to do something, to sacrifice for Him. In school I often went to visit Him and I tried to provide Him with as much joy as possible. All this was done in a hidden way so that no one knew about it, because I confided it to no one. I thought that I could be robbed of all that happiness hidden in my heart.

She was also to write:

The second retreat I made caused many changes. My love was anxious to surrender everything, just so I could be closer to Jesus. My desire began to fly to the very heights of Carmel in which I perceived that highest union with Jesus. I don't know why I yearned for Carmel right from my childhood years, especially since I never knew a Carmelite. I just knew the Carmelite Little Thérèse; I loved her and I wanted to imitate her virtuous life. . . .I did everything with Jesus. I ran to Him with everything, even with the most ordinary things.

One day when Annie was almost fourteen years old, she heard her mother crying and telling a visitor, "But that is a sin against heaven and against the infant . . . you cannot kill it." Annie learned later that a relative had had an abortion. Upon knowing this, Annie spent long hours before Jesus in church offering herself in expiation for sins, especially those of abortion. It was during Holy Week that she offered herself once again to Jesus. She wrote:

> I begged Jesus that he compensate for sins by taking me as his property, that He take my body, my soul, my health, my life, and simply everything that I have. It was during this same Holy Week, on Good Friday, that I was overcome by an attack of coughing, and my handkerchief became red with blood. I was overwhelmed with great happiness. I could do nothing else except to thank Him.

When Sr. Ludmilla learned that Annie had not reported this condition to her mother, she mentioned to Mrs. Zelikova that perhaps Annie should have some X-rays taken. But outwardly, Annie was the picture of health, and so the mother could not understand the sister's request, and Annie was expected to continue her household and farm chores as usual, in addition to her schoolwork. Soon, however, others began to notice Annie's obvious weight loss and her pallid complexion. This time, Sr. Ludmilla persuaded the mother that Annie needed medical attention, and it was Sr. Ludmilla herself who took Annie to see a doctor. The prognosis was not good — advanced tuberculosis. The doctor expressed the opinion that Annie might live three more months, but no longer.

Although the nun was devastated by the news, Annie happily announced with her customary smile, "Christ is soon going to take me to Himself." But Annie was to live not just three months, but four more years, offering everything to Him with great love.

The parents were crushed by the doctor's prognosis and wanted to send Annie to a village in the Tara Mountains, where the clean air was deemed therapeutic. But Annie resisted a move, saying that she was in the hands of God, that she had surrendered herself to Him, and if He willed her to get better, she would do so at home as well as in the mountains. After her request to attend a retreat with the sisters was refused, Sr. Ludmilla asked the retreat preacher, Fr. Hlouch, to visit Annie, which he did. He was so overwhelmed with her spiritual authenticity that he became her spiritual advisor for the rest of her life.

To relieve her parents' anxiety, Annie continued to apply herself to her schoolwork and to her tasks at home and in the fields, but with the beginning of 1939, she began to periodically cough up blood. It was then that they decided to keep her home from school, although she continued to be useful around the house. During this time she wrote down some of her conversations with Jesus, twenty of which have survived. Among other things, the fifteen-year-old wrote:

Dear Jesus, let my love for You be ever greater, and let that love make me forget myself completely. Everything, whether sorrow or joy, comes from Your love. May everything that I am and that I have sing You a song of praise.

Annie dearly missed attending school, where she had often stayed after class to help fellow students with difficult lessons. But she often went to the school during her illness to visit with the students and the sisters. Her last visit took place only a few months before her death. Around this time, she was to write:

How beautiful it is to strive after a strong love, which would look only to give honor and glory to Jesus in everything. Every instant it is possible to give him much — all of one's work, every movement, every word can be uttered with great love. Let us do as much as we can, and when we are unsuccessful in something, let us remain peaceful. It not so much depends on the fruit of our work and effort, but rather on the love which led us to that task.

Annie also gives us this simple way to pray:

When I'm in the woods or in the garden or even before the tabernacle, I call on every blade of grass, on every flower, on every grain of wheat to praise God. I wish I had as many hearts as there are songs of birds, as there are brooks and springs, as many as there are grains, leaves, as many as there are stars and clouds in heaven, so that I could give enough thanks for the gifts of God.

Toward the end of 1939, doctors informed her father that, since her condition was hopeless, they would no longer care for Annie. Annie smiled at the news and was informed by the sisters, "God is the best doctor. He will cure you when He Himself wants to do so." To this, Annie replied, "How beautiful it is that the doctors have given up on me. At least they are not going to interfere with God."

In February of 1940, Annie made a private retreat and recorded expressions that are reminiscent of those made by St. Thérèse:

During this retreat I found true beauty, which is hidden in faithfulness in little things. I always desired to do great and heroic deeds of love, but when I saw that I was unable, I was grieved by it. Now I find great heroism precisely in little things, so that now I haven't the slightest regret whether I can do something or not.

When only fifteen years old, Annie wrote with amazing wisdom to a mother who complained that, with her family duties, her spiritual life was stunted. Part of her letter to this mother reads:

All the care that you dedicate to your little boy, offer it to the Lord Jesus. Have this thought in everything: "I am doing this for Jesus." You could also unite it to the most precious sacrifice of the Lord Jesus on the cross. Even the slightest sacrifice takes on a limitless value. . . . Really, we need not look for sacrifices, since every instant presents us with some. As much work as you must do daily, as many steps, as many words, as many smiles, all of this can be brought lovingly to our beloved Jesus. In the evening you will be amazed at how many flowers of love you picked for Him spontaneously, without being forced. The best thing is right away in the morning to offer Him the whole day with everything that will happen to us.

Annie was finally ordered to bed on December 4, 1940 — only to be forced to leave it frequently when an elderly aunt who lived with the family became sick. Annie was expected to help the family care for this ailing relative, even though she was not feeling well herself and was in considerable pain. But because she looked so well, and performed the chores with her usually pleasant smile, her condition was not considered too serious, and her total confinement to bed was considered perhaps unnecessary.

Annie's spirit of sacrifice is authenticated in her appreciation of her great aunt, who proved to be a trying burden for the whole family. After the aunt passed away, Annie's sister remembered their conversation:

"Dad is glad that now, after the death of Auntie, the family lives in peace as in heaven," she had said.

Annie thought for a moment and then smilingly replied, "Yes, our good God gave us Auntie to help us to practice self-control and strengthen ourselves in virtue. But now this opportunity will be lost to us."

Annie had always felt herself called to be a cloistered Carmelite. When she realized she would not be healed, and that her dream would never be realized, she asked Father Hlouch for permission to admit her to the Third Order Secular of Carmel. Permission was granted from Vienna with a dispensation from the canonical age. After she had made her private vows on February 7, 1941, Annie noted that, for her, life didn't change at all; she had already been living the Carmelite commitment for some time.

Almost echoing the words of St. Thérèse, Annie was to say that she never regretted that she had surrendered herself to the love of Jesus. "I do not regret having sacrificed myself. I will never tell Jesus, 'Let up,' but rather, 'Go ahead.'"

A nun who visited during Annie's last days remembers Annie saying to her, "I must smile to my last breath. Ah, all I can give God now are my heartbeats and my smile. Nothing is left to me except love and trust."

During her last hours on earth, her mother kept vigil with her suffering daughter. As she and the local priest's housekeeper prayed the Sorrowful Mysteries of the rosary, Annie joined them, and when the mother wanted to fetch a cloth to wipe her daughter's feverish forehead, Annie begged her mother to continue praying the rosary with her. Small as the action was, it was yet another offering to Jesus.

The dying eighteen-year-old had always wanted to die with a smile. When it was nearly five o'clock in the morning, a great smile brightened her face and she was heard to exclaim weakly, "How beautiful it all is . . . I wouldn't trade places . . . with anyone." She gazed at the crucifix she held tightly in her hands and kissed it.

Still smiling, she went on, "My heart is beating . . . for Jesus. I love Him so much." After whispering, "I trust," Annie said something else her mother could not understand except for one word — "Carmel." While the morning Angelus bell was chiming, Annie died in the peace of God.

Sr. Ludmilla prepared Annie Zelikova's body for the funeral. It was dressed in white with a laurel wreath and Annie's first Holy Communion veil on her head. A palm was placed at her side, and at her feet was a bouquet of wild roses. Annie's hands fingered her beloved rosary and crucifix, while on her heart was a copy of her first Communion picture, her Carmelite brown scapular, and the Third Order Secular Rule book. Her spiritual advisor, Fr. Joseph Hlouch, conducted the funeral services. During those rites, many people expressed the opinion that Annie Zelikova was truly a saint worthy of imitation. ✝

Blessed Antonia Mesina

1919 – 1935
16 years old
SARDINIA

*A*ntonia was the second born of a family of ten children. She began life in the mountainous interior of Sardinia, in the little city of Orgosolo. Her father, Agostino Mesina, was assigned the guardianship of the rural areas around the community. Antonia's mother, Grazia Raubanu, was noted for her great piety and her appreciation of her daughter, Antonia, whom she called "the flower of my life."

During her infancy and early childhood, Antonia was like all children, being lively and playful as well as obedient and affectionate. When she attended school, she was described as being well liked by both teachers and students. Her instructors noted that Antonia was well behaved, precise, and studious. Always punctual for class, she loved the duties she was asked to perform and exhibited a commendable spirit of sacrifice in bending to the wishes and welfare of her classmates.

At the age of seven, Antonia received her First Holy Communion and, when she was only ten, joined a Catholic Action group. She was proud to be a member and encouraged many to join the group, saying that belonging was a beautiful experience and that it "helps one to be good."

Her mother developed a serious heart condition during Antonia's early school years. Unable to strain herself or lift anything heavy, Grazia became almost totally dependent upon the help of the young Antonia, who was then forced to leave school after attending elementary classes for only four years.

At her tender age, Antonia assumed much of the household chores, helping her mother with cooking, caring for the children, cleaning, and marketing. In addition, washing clothes and carrying water into the house also fell to her charge. It is reported that she performed these and her other responsibilities willingly and diligently, as though she were much older. One of her outstanding virtues was her readiness to renounce her personal pleasures in favor of the needs of the family.

Family members and others who knew her reported that Antonia did her chores joyfully and serenely and accepted the family's modest economic condition, with the hard work and sacrifice this entailed. One would think that Antonia would be less than patient with the other children, considering the many duties she was obliged to perform; but she was affectionate and tender with them, helping them as though she were their mother. She was so submissive and obedient to her parents that her mother proudly claimed, "Antonia never once went against me."

One of Antonia's tasks was the weekly bread baking. This was no easy assignment; she had to grind the grain, sift it, and prepare the dough. One day she asked her friend, Annedda Castangia, to accompany her into the forest while she gathered wood needed for the baking. The day was May 17, 1935, when Antonia was just sixteen years old.

While the two girls were strolling along the path toward the forest, Antonia asked Annedda if she would like to become a member of Catholic Action. When Annedda said she could not afford to join, Antonia was glad to tell her no expenses were involved. She also affirmed the many spiritual benefits to be gained from the good works they performed and the catechetical instruction they received.

What further occurred on that walk through the woods is given in a deposition Annedda gave. She reports that, after gathering a sufficient amount of wood, the girls were preparing to return home when they noticed a teenaged boy along the path. Annedda recognized him as a student from her school, but when he turned onto a different path, the girls thought no more of him. After a time the two girls separated; then Annedda heard Antonia screaming for help.

The youth had sneaked up behind Antonia, grabbed her by the shoulders, and was attempting to force her to the ground. Annedda reported that Antonia broke away twice, but she was caught a third time and knocked down. The would-be rapist then grabbed a large rock and struck Antonia repeatedly on the face and head. Mortally wounded, Antonia continued to gallantly resist.

Horrified by what she saw, Annedda screamed for help and ran to the nearest house. The captain of police was hastily summoned and he, together with other citizens, quickly rode into the forest on horseback. There they found the bloody and brutally wounded body of the sixteen-year-old Antonia. Her face was so horribly disfigured from the fierce beating that they hardly recognized the virtuous little housekeeper.

But after her death, an autopsy determined Antonia's body had not been sinfully violated. Thus, like Maria Goretti, Antonia had died a martyr of holy purity; Annedda identified the assassin, who was captured, tried, and condemned to death.

Some years after Antonia's death, a procession of the townspeople, led by the bishop and several priests, accompanied her relics from the simple grave in the local cemetery to the Church of the Holy Savior, where they now recline in a black marble tomb. Antonia's devotees frequently visit both the tomb and the memorial stone marking the place of her martyrdom.

Pope John Paul II beatified Antonia Mesina on Sunday, October 4, 1987. Also beatified during the same ceremony were Blessed Marcel Callo and Blessed Pierina Morosina — all three being twentieth-century secular people who now await canonization. ✝

Servant of God Antoinetta (Nennolina) Meo

1930 – 1937
6½ years old
R OME

$\mathcal{C}$an a child not yet seven years old — someone not a martyr — attain such a degree of sanctity as to someday be honored on the altars of the church? The Vatican and its learned theologians studied the matter very carefully, but not until 1981 was the matter settled by a declaration of the Sacred Congregation for the Causes of Saints. It affirmed that the Church could fully recognize that children can attain heroic actions of faith, hope, and charity, and thus could be considered for canonization. After reading the story of Nennolina, one can see why the Vatican would vote in the affirmative.

Nennolina was blessed in being born to a prosperous and virtuous family of Rome on December 15, 1930, in a house just a few steps from the Basilica of the Holy Cross in Jerusalem. Nennolina's older sister by eight years, Margherita, reports that Nennolina "was a happy, vivacious, and mischievous child, as are all children her age." When she was three, she attended kindergarten, where the nuns described her as being in "perpetual motion." She loved school and once said that she liked it so much she would willingly attend it at night.

She was not yet five years old when a swelling was noticed on her left knee. It was thought at first that she injured the area in a fall, but when the swelling continued and grew larger, Nennolina suffered a wrong diagnosis. Instead of a proper procedure, the doctor ordered injections of iodine. Nennolina reacted to the first injection with cries and weeping, but when the mother suggested that she think of the sufferings of Jesus, especially the crowning of thorns, the child bore the pain quietly and almost cheerfully.

Eventually the correct diagnosis was made: cancer of the bone. An operation to remove the cancerous leg took place on April 25, 1936, when she was five years and four months old. (Afterward, the surgeon recognized that he might not have operated in time to save the child's life.) Painful medications and fittings for an orthopedic apparatus followed. The doctor described Nennolina's behavior following these procedures and the surgery in this way: "She bore the surgical intervention with uncommon fortitude and with joy, always maintaining herself in a joyful attitude, really unusual for a child of her age." Upon her release from the hospital, in spite of her pain, she continued her life as usual with games and school.

During the month of September 1936, Nennolina suffered from tonsillitis. While she was recuperating, her mother read a book entitled *Holy Children* to her. The book was about little ones from various nationalities who called themselves by different names such as The Patient Little Lamb of Jesus, The Violet of Jesus, and so forth. The mother once asked Nennolina, "And what would you like to be?" Without taking her gaze from a picture of the Sacred Heart in her room, where a candle was always burning, the child answered, "I am the light of Jesus."

During this same convalescence, Padre Orlandi visited and asked the child some questions from the Catechism. He was so impressed with her answers and explanations he suggested that she write or visit the Mother General and ask permission to make her first Communion in their chapel the night of Christmas, 1936, instead of at Easter of 1937.

Nennolina began to anticipate the reception of her first Holy Communion. Her mother helped her study the Catechism in greater detail and took Nennolina to visit the Mother General, as Padre Orlandi had suggested. Nennolina later dictated a note to her mother, who wrote it down and dated it September 15, 1936:

Dear Jesus, I went for a walk today and I went to my nuns and I told them that I want to make my first Communion at Christmas. Jesus, you come soon in my heart so I can hold you strongly and I will kiss you. Jesus, I want you to stay always in my heart.

After a few days more, she dictated:

Dear Jesus, I want you so much. You, I want to repeat it that I want you so much. I give you my heart. Dear *Madonnina*, you are so good. You take my heart and hand it to Jesus.

And then she added something uncommon for a child her age:

My good Jesus, give me some souls, give me so many. I ask gladly. I ask you because you make me become good so I can come with you in Heaven.

This theme, Nennolina would repeat a number of times.

Permission was granted with the reception of her first Holy Communion taking place on Christmas night of 1936, in the chapel of the nuns' convent.

Even before these notes, Nennolina had taken a fancy to letter writing and began dictating other letters to her mother, who dutifully wrote them and placed them under a statuette of the Baby Jesus.

Nennolina's mother explains that the child called these notes "poetries" and wrote them for her father, her sister Margherita, Jesus, and *Madonnina*. For the first letter Nennolina wrote, Madame Meo reports: "I took the first piece of paper that happened to be under my hand and I began to write under dictation, smiling indulgently to what she dictated with so much simplicity and care." Madame Meo admits that, at first, she did not carefully collect these notes and was a bit careless in handling them, because she gave them little importance. Fortunately, a goodly number survived.

These "poetries" number 177 writings of various lengths; 158 of them were published in a book. A few of these were written in her own hand. These show a child of six with an extraordinary mystical ability and a great love of God.

When Nennolina began the first elementary grade, she learned how to use a pen and signed her dictated letters, "Antonietta and Jesus." She once wrote, "My dear Jesus, I have learned today to do it (use the pen), so soon I will write You by myself." Her notes were always finished with embraces, caresses, and kisses. One of the nuns reported that she saw Nennolina going into the church, where she knelt down and exclaimed, "Jesus, You come to play with me." And in some of her letters she would say, "Dear Jesus, come tomorrow to school with me."

On the eve of her first Communion, she dictated this little note:

Dear Jesus, tomorrow when You will be in my heart, make account that my soul is an apple. And, as in the apple there are seeds, just as You put in my soul. And, as the bottom of the black peel of the seeds, as they are in us, the inside of the seed is white, so also inside the soul there is your grace that would be as the white seed.

Her mother asked if the sisters had used this as an example in school to demonstrate grace in the soul. Nennolina replied, "No, mother. I have thought it by myself."

And Nennolina thought of poor sinners on a number of occasions, as demonstrated by this letter: "I pray to You for that man who has been so bad. I pray that You know that he is very old and is in the hospital of St. Giovanni."

After Nennolina received the sacrament of Confirmation, her condition became progressively worse. She developed a cough and, because of weakness, was confined to bed. In spite of this pain, however, she always remarked, "But I am well." She always wanted to recite her usual morning and evening prayers and asked for Holy Communion, after which she became stronger and more placid.

Her devotions were many. She loved to recite the Holy Rosary, make novenas, and pray for the conversion of sinners and the souls in Purgatory. But above all, she loved the Redeemer and wanted to console Him. This concern for Him and her utter simplicity and holiness are displayed in this "poetry":

Dear Jesus, if You were only a man and I locked You inside a house, You would not feel the offenses that are done you. And, so, You could come in my heart and stay locked within me. And I will make You so many sacrifices and I will tell You some stories to console you.

It was a "poetry" such as this that stirred Padre Garrigou-Lagrange to declare:

She has given testimony, considering her tender age, of an understanding, of a love of the redeeming suffering that cannot be explained without recognizing the intervention of extraordinary graces.

It was also this learned prelate who declared that Nennolina was already contemplative and experienced the "prayer of simplicity."

Her last letter was written on June 2, a letter that found its way into the hands of Pope Pius XI. The mother describes how she took a seat close to the bed and wrote what Antoinetta dictated. The note reads:

Dear crucified Jesus. I want You so much and I love You so much. I want to be with You on Calvary and I suffer with joy because I know I am on Calvary. Dear Jesus, I thank You that You have sent me this illness because it is a means to arrive in Heaven . . . Dear Jesus, tell Padre God that I also love Him so much. Dear Jesus, give me the strength to bear these pains that I offer You for sinners.

Her mother reports that here, Nennolina began to cough violently and to vomit. When she recovered enough to continue, she went on.

Dear Jesus, tell the Holy Spirit that illuminates me of love and gives me the seven gifts. Dear Jesus, tell the *Madonnina* that I love her so much and I want to be near her on Calvary because I want to be your victim of love. Dear Jesus, I want to repeat that I love You so much, so much. My Good Jesus, I recommend to You my spiritual father and give him necessary graces. Dear Jesus, I recommend my parents and Margherita. Your child sends You so many kisses.

The mother reports that she felt a sense of rebellion seeing how the child suffered. Angry, she rolled up the paper and threw it in a drawer.

A few days later, a professor from the University of Milan was called for a consultation, since one more surgery had been ordered. He spoke with the patient and was amazed that, even in such pain, she was cheerful and uncomplaining. During the visit, Nennolina's father also mentioned the letters to him. After seeing the last one, the professor felt the Holy Father should be told about the child. Since the professor knew the pontiff, he took the letter to him.

The following day, an envoy arrived to present Nennolina with the apostolic blessing. He told the family that the Holy Father, touched by the letter, had asked to be recommended to Nennolina's prayers.

The child became progressively worse, needing an extraction of fluid from her lungs, and the adjustment of three ribs under local anesthetic. After this procedure, the doctor reported: "Antoniette tightened her teeth, the face contracted, and she was seen to struggle against a whimper, but she never complained." Those who witnessed the procedure also remarked, "She bore it all with heroic fortitude, always having a little smile even among the greatest pains." It was soon after these procedures that Nennolina turned to her mother and predicted the time of her death, saying, "Mother, be happy. I will go out from here in ten days."

In the time that followed, despite her cancer, she continued to smile at the nurses who came to tend her wounds. Large tumors compressed her lungs to the point of involving the heart, causing a continuous suffocation and irritation of the throat. She then suffered from cancer of the brain, a hand, and a foot, as well as thrush to the mouth and the throat; but the principal source of suffering, permanent and increasing, was the lungs. After a time, the child became so calm and pleasant that her mother asked the doctors about her demeanor, saying, "Doctor, I don't believe it . . . tell me, does Antonietta suffer?"

The doctor replied, "But lady, what do you ask . . . ? Her pains are atrocious."

The mother said she then went to Antonietta and told her she wanted a blessing. With her little hand, the girl traced a small cross on her mother's forehead.

When the father proposed that she receive the last sacraments that might bring health to the body, Nennolina listened, but when the priest explained that the sacraments gave graces to the soul, she answered, "Yes, I want it." She calmly responded to all the prayers, and at the end, she kissed the crucifix of her first Holy Communion. It is said that all took place in simplicity and peace.

Exactly ten days later, the First Saturday of the month, just as she had predicted, Nennolina died on July 3, 1937. Before her last breath she whispered, "Jesus, Maria, mother, dad . . ." She fixed her gaze in front of her, smiled, then exhaled for the last time. She was exactly six years, six months and nineteen days old.

The next day her little coffin was taken to the Basilica of the Holy Cross in Jerusalem where the relics of the Passion of Our Lord are kept, and the same church where the child had been baptized. After her funeral service her little casket was taken to the local cemetery.

Following the burial, the family received messages from people of great distinction, including Msgr. Giovanni Battista Montini, the future Pope Paul VI; Rev. Agostino Gemelli; the Rev. Reginald Garrigou-Lagrange; and the national president of the Female Youth of Catholic Action, (future) Servant of God Armida Barelli. In a letter dated December 20, 1941, Armida announced that the national center of Catholic Action would assume the Cause of Nennolina's Beatification — this because she had belonged to the children's division of the group. Other letters of condolence came from bishops, archbishops, and members of the clergy who held positions of importance.

The Cause for Nennolina's Beatification was introduced in 1972. Her little remains were transferred from the cemetery to the Basilica of the Holy Cross of Jerusalem on May 3, 1999, where they are now kept.

In one of her last letters, Nennolina wrote:

> Dear Eucharistic Jesus, when You will come in my heart with your graces in the closet of my soul for the last time, you will find many sacrifices. And when you will come for the last time in my heart I will be soon dead and will make my soul fly to Heaven where You and your Father and the Holy Spirit and the dear *Madonnina* will be. I will want to enjoy you!

There is no doubt that this child is now enjoying the heavenly ones she so dearly loved during her brief time on earth. ✝

Servant of God Bernard Lehner

1930 – 1944
14 years old
GERMANY

$\mathcal{B}$orn in Herrngiersdorf, the son of a carpenter, Bernard was a studious, religious boy whose love for all things sacred led him to attend the seminary school in Regensburg when he was thirteen years old. All went well with his studies, and his increase in virtue, until he contracted septic diphtheria. He was taken to the children's clinic of the city, where he seemed to improve; however, at Christmastime, his condition worsened with the onset of paralysis.

He was an ideal patient. Doctors, nurses, and visitors were amazed that he willingly accepted bitter medicine and medical procedures without complaint, offering the sacrifices for the saving of souls and the good of the church. Other patients' visitors soon learned of the brave and virtuous young boy and began to visit him as well as their own loved ones. He willingly and cheerfully greeted everyone and accepted many requests for his prayers. His serene courage in the face of pain and various complications was amazing to all; at this time, many already considered him a saint, especially when he began to demonstrate healing powers and help others in their illnesses.

After ten weeks of intense suffering, Bernard realized that he was about to die and requested the Sacrament of the Sick. He told the priest, and all who loved him, "I will soon die, but do not cry since I am going to heaven." He was perfectly conscious on January 24, 1944, when he contentedly accepted death as his joyous entrance into the kingdom of God.

Many grieved at his passing, including the priests of the seminary, who attended the funeral. With family and friends accompanying the youngster's casket, he was buried in the cemetery of Herrngiersdorf.

One might expect that, dying as he did during the height of World War II in Germany, Bernard and his saintliness in the face of suffering and death would have been forgotten — especially during the poverty and tribulations after the war. However, the opposite seemed to be the case. Such was the love and devotion of his memory that his story spread throughout Europe, eventually coming to the attention of church authorities.

In early 1948, Archbishop Michele Buchberger of Regensburg studied the case of Bernard Lehner and opened the process for the child's beatification. After all the necessary preparations were completed, the Cause was officially initiated in 1950, just six years after Bernard's death. In the presence of church representatives, 39 witnesses were questioned, including eight companions of Bernard and the doctors who had cared for him. In 1951, the documents relating to the case were submitted to the Congregation for the Causes of Saints.

Soon after Bernard's death, one of the priests of the seminary, the Jesuit Giuseppe Kunz, wrote a small biography published in 1947. This also helped in spreading the saintliness of this young teenager.

Two years after the initial opening of the Cause, on September 12, 1952, the translation of Bernard's remains took place. Accompanying the relics from the cemetery to the church of the city were 20,000 people who extolled the boy as a saint. ✝

Blessed Caroline Kozka

1898 − 1914
16 years old
POLAND

When Nazi Germany and Russian forces invaded Poland in September 1939 and divided the country, the military forces of both countries were ruthless. The Communist government of Russia, who claimed the eastern part of Poland, was every bit the equal of Hitler, who ordered the closing of schools, colleges, publishing houses, and printing presses. They closed churches and arrested priests and religious. Polish men were forcibly drafted into the German army, and countless citizens were harassed or executed. It has been estimated that the Nazis killed six million Polish citizens, half of them Jews.

One Polish casualty of the war was sixteen-year-old Caroline Kozka whose village of Wal-Ruda was in the Russian-occupied part of the country. She was the fourth of the eleven children of Jan and Maria Borzecka Kozka, who lived in a devout rural community. The children were raised as Catholics, with Caroline attending Holy Mass and devotional services. She also taught Catechism at the local parish church, the center of the community's life.

At the age of sixteen, Caroline was attractive and full of life, with enthusiasm for her future. A Russian soldier interrupted her dreams when he grabbed Caroline as she was walking through the village. He pulled her into the woods and attempted to rape her. She struggled valiantly, so much so that he became furious with her repeated rejections. In anger, he mercilessly beat her, finally crushing her skull with the butt of his rifle. The date was November 18, 1914.

When Caroline did not return home, her family and fellow villagers conducted a frantic search. Some 17 days later, on December 4, the pitifully mangled body was discovered. Two days later the little virgin was buried in the parish cemetery at Zabawa.

Three years later, a cross was erected at the place of her martyrdom. Caroline Kozka has always been regarded as a martyr of purity.

During a visit in Tarnow, Poland, on June 10, 1987, Pope John Paul II beatified the little sixteen-year-old, mentioning during the ceremony that the teenager, in her purity, refused to surrender it to lustful demands even at the cost of her life. ✝

Chiara (Luce) Badano

〜⚭〜

1971 – 1990
18 years old
ITALY

*H*er parents had to wait eleven years before this first child was born, and when she came on October 29, 1971, she was greeted with tremendous love and pride and a great deal of family attention. Her father, Ruggero, was a truck driver in Sassello, near Genoa. When the child was born, her mother, Maria Teresa, left her factory job to care for the baby. Their household was happy and pious, which produced a happy and pious child. And, although they dearly loved Chiara, these wise parents did not let her exceed the limits of proper behavior.

She was a good child, even if sometimes her self-determination got in the way. Once, she was asked to help clear the dishes. She merely replied, "No, I don't want to," and walked away. But after a moment, she returned and willingly helped her mother, saying that she did so because of a lesson she had learned in a Bible story. This and other small incidents present a realistic picture of Chiara as a normal child.

But already in the first grade, she demonstrated a generous and loving nature: during a Christmas assignment, she wrote to the Infant Jesus, "Please make Grandma and all those who are sick get better."

Her spiritual upbringing was solidly Catholic, begun in the home and extended to an active parish community including interesting CCD classes and the influence of a holy pastor. Her spiritual formation was greatly enhanced when, in September 1980 — at the age of nine — she was introduced to the Focolare movement and began attending meetings designed for children her age. (The movement even influenced her parents, who derived great spiritual benefits from it as well.) Chiara was especially attracted to the elderly and always tried to help them. She was also mindful of her classmates and assisted them when she could.

It is said that, as an adolescent, Chiara radiated a spiritual beauty. She was a very attractive girl of delicate features, a winsome smile, and beautiful, luminous eyes.

When she became a teenager, her parents moved to a larger city, Savona, so that she could attend high school. (Chiara could not boast that she was a good student; much to her disappointment, she failed the first year.) As a high school student she was a typical teenager, with a love of song and dance. She was especially fond of joining her friends at the local coffee shop at night, despite having to maintain a strict curfew set by her parents — although not without some protest! She liked pretty clothes and, now and then, noticed and remarked about certain of the high school boys. She seems to have been like all girls her age except that, even then, she was experiencing a deep spiritual life.

During the summer of 1988, she accompanied a group of Focolare children to Rome and wrote home:

Something very important happened here. I encountered Jesus crucified and forsaken . . . Chiara Lubich (the foundress and president of the Focolare Movement) explained to us that He has to be the spouse of our souls.

After that meeting, Chiara began to correspond with Chiara Lubich and even asked her to recommend a new name for her new spiritual life. She was given the name *Chiara Luce,* meaning "Chiara Light." From then on, she was affectionately known by this name.

The two Chiaras corresponded until the teenager's death. The foundress' letters helped her enormously, which enabled her to say at the end of her life, "All I have I owe to God and to Chiara Lubich."

Chiara Luce loved sports, particularly tennis; during one of her practice sessions, however, she felt a severe pain in her shoulder. When it persisted, it was diagnosed as osteosarcoma with metastasis, a very painful form of cancer. She and her parents accepted the news courageously, with Chiara Luce later saying that Jesus had sent the sickness at the right moment.

At the beginning of her confinement, some of the Focolare children visited her, but according to one of them, "In a short time we realized that we couldn't do without her. She attracted us like a magnet." Even her doctors were impressed with her patience and pleasant attitude.

Chiara Luce underwent two operations, followed by chemotherapy, but her mind seemed always to be on the will of God. As each drop fell from the intravenous bottle, she would whisper, "For you, Jesus." She once remarked, "What is this drop in comparison with the nails in Jesus' hands?"

She also lost her hair but, once again, this did not upset her; as each clump fell, she merely said, "For you, Jesus." Everything was for Jesus, including her small savings, which she gave to a friend going to Africa to do missionary work. She told him, "I don't need this money anymore. I have everything." Even when she lost the use of her legs, she took it with equanimity. "If I had to choose between walking again or going to heaven," she said, " I would choose heaven without hesitation."

She refused to accept morphine, saying that she wanted to remain clear-headed so that she could offer her pain to Jesus. "I want to share a little bit of his cross with him."

When Chiara Luce was stricken with a severe hemorrhage in July of 1989, although she recovered from it, she realized the end was near. She cautioned her parents not to cry for her, since she was going to Jesus, then added, "At my funeral, I don't want people to cry, I want them to sing." She referred to her funeral as the "wedding feast" and asked to be dressed as a bride. She chose the songs and even the readings for her funeral Mass. And she advised her mother, "Think when you are dressing me, 'Chiara Luce now sees Jesus.'" All who came in contact with her remarked that Chiara Luce had an impressive spiritual maturity for one of her age. Even the cardinal of her city, hearing of her reputation for holiness, came to visit her. When he asked why her eyes seemed so intensely luminous, she just replied, "I try to love Jesus a lot!"

Finally, on October 7, 1990, Chiara Luce died peacefully with her parents beside her and her friends nearby. Her last words were: "Goodbye, Mom. Be happy, because I'm very happy."

More than 2,000 people attended the funeral, conducted by the local bishop. He said in his homily, "She is the fruit of a Christian family, of a Christian community, and of a movement where mutual love is lived, and where Jesus is present."

Books about Chiara Luce are in preparation, as is the Cause for her Beatification started by Bishop Livio Maritano. Asked why he was so interested in the life of this young girl, he responded:

> I thought that her example could be very meaningful for young people today. It's enough to consider how she lived the experience of her illness, and to see the effects of her death. Sanctity is needed today. And we have to help young people give their lives focus; overcome uncertainty, loneliness, and questions, especially when they encounter disappointment, suffering, and death. Theories are not enough. What is needed is a living example such as the one she left. +

Blessed David Okelo and Blessed Jildo Irwa

17 and 12 years old
d. 1918
UGANDA

When the Catholic missionaries arrived in the region of Kitgum, Uganda, in 1915, many of the natives converted quickly. But challenges followed just as quickly: the advent of World War I, a smallpox breakout that resulted in the scarcity of medicines and food, tribal infighting, and anti-Christian colonists who feared that Christians would interfere with their ivory trade. Christianity, they reasoned, would prove to be an obstacle for their business.

From the midst of these difficulties emerged two martyrs, David Okelo and Jildo Irwa. They belonged to the Acholi tribe, whose members still live in northern Uganda and other parts of Africa. The birth dates of the two are uncertain, but it is known that they both were baptized on June 1, 1916, and confirmed on October 15 of the same year.

After attending catechetical school, the two friends journeyed to the region known as Paimol to continue the catechetical work that David's brother, Antonio, had begun before he was cruelly killed. The missionaries tried to dissuade the two boys, saying that the region was dangerous, and that they would probably be killed as well. But the two brave little catechists replied, "If they kill us, we will go to Paradise. Antonio is already there. We do not fear to die. Jesus will be with us."

They arrived at their destination in November 1917 and began their mission of evangelization at once. At dawn each day, David called his catechumens to prayer. Together with Jildo, they said the rosary, and taught prayers, as well as the questions and answers of the Catechism. In addition, they visited neighboring villages and helped the parents of the catechumens in the fields or with the cattle. In the evening, they again had prayer in common and the recitation of the rosary, concluding it with a song to the Blessed Virgin. Sunday was a special day with services attended by the catechumens and catechists of other areas.

Eleven months after the two young catechists' arrival, local chiefs confronted them and demanded that they abandon teaching the Gospel. Reluctant to kill the young boys, the chiefs instead wanted a bargain: if David and Jildo left the region and stopped the teaching of the Catholic religion, their lives would be spared. But both boys refused. As Jildo replied to this proposal, "We have worked together. If it is necessary to die, we will have to die together."

The warriors wanted to avoid opposition from the natives. So, under cover of darkness one night, four men crept into the huts where the boys slept and dragged them out of the village. David was the first to die. It was then Jildo's turn. Turning to one of the killers, who seemed unwilling to harm him, Jildo merely said, "As many times as you have struck David, you must do to me, since we were together in teaching the faith." Thus, shortly before dawn on October 19, 1918, they were speared and knifed to death in Palamuku, Uganda, their bodies dragged by ropes into the forest and left unattended for several days. When the bodies were discovered, the natives were amazed that vultures or the beasts of the forest had not attacked them. The place of their deaths has since been called *Wi-Polo*, meaning "in Heaven."

Their remains were first buried in simple graves; then, in 1926, the apostolic prefect of north Uganda, Msgr. Antonio Vignato, had the remains taken to the parish church of Kitgum where they were entombed.

At the time of their martyrdom, David was between sixteen and eighteen years of age; Jildo was between twelve and fourteen. David is remembered as a person of gentle character, timid, diligent in his tasks as catechist, and liked by all. He never involved himself in tribal or political disputes. Father Gambaretto, who administered the sacraments to both boys, described the younger Jildo as a person of sweet character, cheerful and very intelligent, always eager to join David in whatever had to be done, and conscientious in conducting his catechetical classes.

In 1952, the Church began the official investigation into the heroic nature of the martyrdom, followed by the publication of books detailing the events. All the papers relating to the two martyrs were delivered to the Congregation for the Causes of Saints in April 1999.

The Christians of the area still recall with reverence the heroic deaths of their catechists. Without exception, they praise the boys for all the good they did in the fulfillment of their mission and their steadfast adherence to their faith. Pope John Paul II, who beatified the two boys on October 20, 2002, also praised their lives and the manner of their deaths. +

Servant of God Faustino Perez-Manglano

⸺⸺∞⸺⸺

1946 – 1963
16 years old
SPAIN

$\mathcal{H}$e was born when the world was just recovering from the Second World War and lived during the time of Vatican II. He rode a school bus during his early grades, occasionally watched the "telly," and was an all-around normal boy. He loved reading good novels, hiking, climbing mountains, swimming, camping, and sleeping in tents. He enjoyed sports, but was particularly fond of soccer and the National Valencia Team, and rarely missed his school's sports competitions. He studied judo for a time, and even indulged in a little slang, writing after he failed a math test, "What a drag." He was well adjusted, fun loving, a good student, and popular with his peers. As his friends were later to say of him, "He was always smiling." Could such a boy achieve sanctity in only sixteen years? Apparently the Church believes he did; his Cause for Beatification was introduced in 1986, only 23 years after his death.

Faustino was the son of a doctor, Faustino senior, and Encarna, his mother, who welcomed other children into their family: Marie

Encarna in 1948, Eugenia in 1950, and Joaquin in 1956. Born in Valencia, Spain, Faustino was baptized at the font where the great St. Vincent Ferrer had also been baptized. He received the Sacrament of Confirmation in 1955.

When he was only four, Faustino attended the Loreto school, conducted by the Sisters of the Holy Family, but when he was six he transferred to Our Lady of the Pillar, run by the Marianist Order. He was a good student — not especially brilliant, but he applied himself and received an award for Extraordinary Application in 1956.

During the school year of 1957-58, his teacher gave individual "character analyses" of the students. Faustino's reads, in part:

> Small, but serious, a worker, respectful and amiable. Faustino is a thoroughly good boy. Without much aptitude for sports, he prefers to amuse himself in other ways. He is very talented, has a good memory and easy, sustained attention. To this he adds enthusiastic and joyful work. His moral side is no less inspiring: a lover of peace, without noise and shouting, simple and refined in his dealings. His soul is pure and transparent, open to the noblest sentiments, docile and sincerely pious. This is why he can experience the happiness that comes from being good.

If he was already a good boy, his virtues would increase much more beginning in 1959, when he was thirteen and in the eighth grade. It was then that he made his first retreat, an impetus for him to "change my life completely." In his notes he made simple summaries of the talks, and these reveal that they made a deep impression.

It was during this retreat that he consulted his spiritual director about a problem. He explained: "When I was in the fifth grade I promised the Virgin to pray the rosary every day until 1961. And I am praying, especially when I go alone to school . . . but I forget sometimes . . . and I try to catch up little by little."

The spiritual director asked if he liked to pray the rosary.

"Yes, Father," he replied. "A lot."

Hearing this, the spiritual director wisely lifted the young man's burden and recommended that he pray the rosary whenever he was able.

A spiritual treasure left for us is a diary Faustino started in the summer of 1960. In it can be seen the steady progress he made in his love of the Blessed Virgin and Our Lord. His love of the rosary is repeated throughout as, for example, the September 14, 1960, entry: "I finished the *Mario Gaitan*. A beautiful book... At quarter to nine, I prayed the rosary."

Again he wrote, on October 3: "School started. I heard Mass and went to Communion. I prayed the whole rosary..."

Mention of the rosary is woven throughout the entries.

Faustino was a dedicated fan of the Valencia soccer team, also mentioned throughout the diary. When he conversed with Jesus he even mentioned the scores of the games, as he did in his entry of October 10, displaying his utter simplicity and naturalness in prayer: "I prayed the rosary. I went to Communion during recreation... I talked ten minutes with Christ about the Zaragoza-Valencia tie (a soccer game) and the missions."

Another time he wrote, "I prayed the rosary, and went to Communion. We won the soccer game 10-3. I spoke ten minutes with Christ..."

In November 1960, Faustino had surgery under his arm for the removal of a cystic tumor that had made him very ill and caused pain for almost a year. Unable to attend school, he nevertheless studied at home, when the pain permitted, and received radiotherapy treatments. In early 1961, however, he received an alarming diagnosis: an apparent malignant infection of the lymph glands. Later, suffering from a sharp pain in the lumbar region, he went with his father to see a radiologist. The doctor's report states:

The x-ray showed a vertebra being pressured by a tumor. The diagnosis was confirmed by further studies. He had Hodgkin's disease in a fatal form. . . . Faustino was a quiet, serious, sincere, and suffering child. I never heard him complain . . .

It was a long and burdensome sickness, but the doctor reported, "With radiotherapy and chemotherapy, he got better right away."

After the treatments, Faustino became bloated and lost all his hair. When asked by his spiritual director if he minded being seen like that, he answered with a laugh, "There's nothing bad about it. If your hair falls out, what are you going to do? It will grow back. What went away will come back again." Faustino was not one to worry about what he considered to be trivial matters.

Some time later, he was well enough to return to school and attend a retreat; it was during that retreat that he decided to consecrate his life to God as a Marianist priest. From that day onward this desire grew, evidenced by numerous entries in his diary displaying his joy at offering his life to Jesus and the Church. One entry reads, "I'm about to burst with immense happiness. How marvelous Christ is!" In his diary, he speaks of his vocation forty-two times.

Another entry shows the naturalness of this boy:

I prayed the rosary. I went to Communion during recreation. I was called on during math class and knew the answers well. In drawing, 80%. The league standing (the Valencia soccer team) is now 8 for them and 0 for us. It's difficult to stop quarreling with my sisters. The vocation is clearer every day. I want to be a Marianist religious with a degree in chemistry.

His love of the Blessed Mother prompted the family to make a quick visit to Zaragoza, to Our Lady of the Pillar, a beloved shrine of the Marianist Order. He was to write of his visit,

We went to the Marianist scholasticate . . . I liked my future home. Every day I love the Mother, the Virgin Mary, more. I prayed for three things (during the visit to the shrine), my vocation, that papa will have work, and I thanked her for my cure. How marvelous the Virgin of the Pillar is!

Faustino was even well enough to journey to Lourdes for a few days, where he found time to serve as a *brancardier,* or stretcher-bearer, helping at the pools and at the Grotto. During his return to Valencia, his love for the sick and suffering was noted in his diary: "The next time I go to Lourdes I will go as a stretcher-bearer." He did not receive a cure at the shrine of Our Lady of the Pillar nor at Lourdes, but he did receive a reserve of energy that helped during school time.

Faustino's endurance for suffering and self-denial, as well as his desire to please others, showed when he visited his grandparents in Alicante. His grandmother recalls that at every meal, he was given a glass of milk with *Cola-cao.* "He drank many cans of it in the month he was in the house." Sometime later, when his cousins were telling what drink they liked most, some mentioned coffee with milk; another, a certain cereal drink. Without thinking, Faustino said, "What I can't stand is *Cola-cao.* It makes me nauseous."

On hearing that, the grandmother remarked, "But why didn't you tell me?"

"Grandma," he answered, "you did it with so much pleasure that I didn't want to deprive you of the enjoyment."

Faustino also showed a lively interest in others' welfare. When the maid received a raise in salary, he thanked his mother. Although living in comfortable surroundings, he was concerned for others, especially the poor. Once, he heard about a fourteen-year-old boy who lived in a small attic; he was told the boy had nothing to eat, was poorly clothed, and worked eight hours a day at a bar. Then and there, Faustino decided, "We're going to buy this boy a shirt, or else they'll throw him out of the bar."

In fact, he bought the boy two shirts. Faustino also talked with him, tried to find other work for him, and helped him in many friendly ways. A note in the diary reads that Faustino brought the boy "food, clothes, a package, and some medicine."

His last camping trip took place in 1962 and lasted 20 days. Among other places, he and his group visited Zaragoza, Pamplona, Chartres, Paris, and the Swiss Alps. Summarizing the trip in a letter, he wrote, "I enjoyed the trip very much. I liked everything, and since I am quiet and like the country, there was nothing like Planchouet . . . I think these days have helped me to sacrifice myself more for others. I tried to be as helpful as possible."

His companions on the trip stated that Faustino "was above all a serviceable boy." Another wrote, "He was always ready to do a favor. . . . He had one of the virtues I admire most: charity."

Another companion on the trip wrote:

I was his companion in the tent and on the bus. He was always the same; never angry, always ready to sacrifice himself, to do with something worse so others could have something better. I firmly believe that when a person has some defect, where you see it most is in camping. I can say only that after twenty days of sleeping and eating with him, I didn't find any defect.

The opening of another school year coincided with the first session of Vatican Council II and, unfortunately, the return of his sickness. Because he was so weak, his mother had to help dress him and comb his hair. When ready, he was placed in a taxi to be taken to school. This was repeated day after day. One friend commented, "What impressed me most was his capacity for suffering. When I found out that they even had to dress him, and he studied in bed, I was astonished. That was when I realized how much he had to suffer. He never said, 'I'm in pain today,' and I never noticed it."

Faustino smiled through it all, even though phlebitis pained both legs. By January 1963, he was worse. Those who saw him found it hard to watch him dragging himself from one place to another, bent over like an old man — yet he was still smiling.

At his last retreat, he apparently felt some presentiment of his coming death, as he entered in his diary:

We must accept death as of now. A death with the Virgin is marvelous. Christ, grant that every day I may be more devoted to Mary. I want to be always intimately united to her. She will help me to die, and I will have the death of a true saint. . . . Welcome to our sister, death.

Soon after that he wrote, "I am very happy. I want to suffer for Christ who suffered so much for me. I must become a saint. My presence must give witness to Christ." When asked by his spiritual director if he was suffering a great deal, he commented, "Father, I think that right now there are others who are suffering much more than I am."

On a table beside his bed was a sheet of paper on which he had copied a series of quotations about suffering bravely for Christ. He told his mother that he wanted it always close by so that he could read it. (Despite this knowledge of his own coming death, however, his interest in soccer never waned. On the reverse side of the paper, he had written the proposed plan of the National Soccer Team!)

As his death approached, he also often voiced his disappointment at not becoming a Marianist; because of the seriousness of his condition, the Marianist General Administration, hearing of this, admitted Faustino to the novitiate to allow him to profess vows in *articulo mortis* (in a dying condition), and so he became a Marianist after all. He received Holy Communion every day though suffering grievously, his body greatly swollen. Finally — on March 3, 1963 — the day arrived for his entrance into heaven. With a medal of the Blessed Virgin in his hand, he died in the arms of his mother.

His reputation of sanctity led to the introduction of his Cause for Beatification. As a first step, on April 11, 1986, his remains were transferred from the general cemetery in Valencia to the chapel of Our Lady of the Pillar school.

The following entry in Faustino's diary was written on January 25, 1962:

Sanctity is very difficult.

But I will try, and who knows if I might achieve it?

Those who knew Faustino, or even just knew of him, pray that the desire expressed in this entry will be fulfilled, and that he will someday be honored on the altars of the Church. +

Blessed Francisco Marto

1908 – 1919
11 years old
PORTUGAL

This visionary of Our Lady of Fátima was a very quiet little boy, very agreeable — and always, it seems, trailing his little sister Jacinta and cousin Lucia wherever they went. He spoke very little, just did everything he saw Jacinta and Lucia doing, rarely suggesting anything himself. He was even-tempered, trusting, affectionate, entirely guileless and humble, demonstrating a quiet, submissive, and placid nature. It is said that he inherited these traits from his father, who possessed the same qualities.

Lucia, the oldest of the three children, wrote of him: "I must confess that I myself did not always feel too kindly disposed towards him as his naturally calm temperament exasperated my own excessive vivacity." And again: "In our games he was quite lively, but not many of us liked to play with him as he nearly always lost. If one of the other children insisted on taking away from him something that belonged to him, he would say: 'Let them have it! What do I care?'"

An incident of this nature took place one day when he showed a group of children a handkerchief with a picture of Our Lady of Nazare that someone had given him. Everyone admired it, passing it from one to another; then, in a few moments, the handkerchief seemed to disappear. Lucia found it in the pocket of a small boy and attempted to take it from him, but the boy insisted it was his. To settle the matter, Francisco went up to the boy and said, "Let him have it! What does a handkerchief matter to me?"

His temperament was well suited to his life as a shepherd and his deep love of living things and nature, befitting a boy whose patron was St. Francis of Assisi. His love of quiet and solitude also led him to prefer being alone, playing his flute, while Lucia and Jacinta amused themselves with games. He must have been somewhat proficient with his playing, since Jacinta would sway and dance to his tunes.

Lucia notes that Francisco loved the birds and enjoyed throwing crumbs for them to eat. He was troubled when someone robbed the nests and distressed when he saw a young boy holding a bird in his hand. After paying two coins for the bird, Francisco let it go, warning the bird not to be caught again.

Among many virtues Francisco displayed was the compassion he showed toward an old woman known as Ti Maria Careira, who shepherded her own flock of goats and sheep. Lucia relates that her animals were rather wild and often strayed, to Ti Maria's great confusion. Francisco was the first to run and help her, leading the flock to pasture and gathering them together for the journey back home. Overwhelmed with gratitude, the old woman called him her "dear guardian angel."

(After the apparition, when the sick came to ask his prayers, his compassion was again aroused. He would tell Jacinta or Lucia: "I can't bear to see them, as I feel so sorry for them. Tell them I'll pray for them.")

Francisco's deep humility was demonstrated at the first apparition of Our Lady, when he alone could not hear the words spoken by the heavenly visitor. He never felt slighted by this, but instead, quietly asked his companions what was said. Again, his feelings could have been severely wounded when Our Lady told Jacinta and Lucia they would go to heaven, but Francisco? "He will go there too, but he must say many rosaries." Francisco could have questioned why he was the only one singled out in this way. Instead, he replied, humbly but enthusiastically, "Oh, my dear Lady! I will say as many rosaries as you want."

Before the children experienced the vision of hell, they were discussing one day all the requests made by the Lady and were wondering how they were to make sacrifices. It was Francisco who suggested, "Let us give our lunch to the sheep and make the sacrifice of doing without it." All agreed, and the contents of their lunch bags were quickly spread among the sheep.

On days when they gave away their lunches, it was Francisco who found a substitute. Climbing swiftly up the holm oaks and other oak tree varieties in the meadow where their sheep grazed, Francisco filled his pockets with acorns. When they realized that the oak trees produced the more bitter acorns than holm oaks, they ate these in sacrifice for sinners.

One day, in the middle of summer, the three shepherds were exceedingly thirsty. Noticing a house nearby, they knocked on the door and were met by a little old woman who gave them a pitcher of water and some bread, which Lucia accepted gratefully. She offered it first to Francisco; he in turn reminded them of the sacrifice they should make by refusing to drink, saying, "I want to suffer for the conversion of sinners." In imitation of Francisco, both Jacinta and Lucia both declined to drink. Instead, Lucia poured the water in the hollow of a rock for the sheep.

Once, when Jacinta was weakened from lack of food and drink, she asked Lucia to make the crickets and the frogs keep quiet because she had a terrible headache. Instead, Francisco asked her, "Don't you want to suffer this for sinners?"

Considering that, Jacinta replied, "Yes, I do. Let them sing."

Francisco also protected his sister when they were together in the prison at Ourem. Jacinta, feeling abandoned by her parents, began to cry, but Francisco promptly encouraged her, saying, "Don't cry. We can offer this to Jesus for sinners." Then, raising his eyes and hands to heaven, he made the offering:

"O my Jesus, this is for love of You, and for the conversion of sinners."

From all accounts, this mild-mannered boy showed surprising courage in prison. In trying to cheer Jacinta when she felt homesick, he told his sister, "Even if we never see our mother again, let us be patient! We can offer it for the conversion of sinners. The worst thing would be if Our Lady never came back again! This is what hurts me most. But I offer this as well for sinners. . . . I miss Our Lady so much."

When the children were praying with the prisoners and Francisco saw that one of the kneeling prisoners still had his hat on, he quietly went up to the man and said, "If you wish to pray, you should take your cap off." The man immediately removed it and handed the cap to Francisco who placed it on the bench atop his own cap.

And then while Jacinta was being questioned in another room, Francisco went up to Lucia and, with great joy, confided, "If they kill us as they say, we'll soon be in heaven! How wonderful! Nothing else matters!"

After the prison experience, Francisco often left his two companions and seemed to disappear, only to be found kneeling behind a little wall or a bush. His only reason for doing so was because "I prefer to pray alone . . . so that I can think and console Our Lord who is so sad." Lucia once asked him, "Francisco, which do you like better — to console Our Lord or to convert sinners, so that no more souls will go to hell?" To this he replied, "I would rather console Our Lord. Didn't you notice how sad Our Lady was last month, when she said that people must not offend Our Lord any more, for He is already much offended? I would like to console Our Lord, and after that convert sinners, so that they won't offend Him any more."

Offering sacrifices seemed to be always on his mind, as it was one day when Lucia's godmother offered the three children a mead drink. She handed the first glass to Francisco, but he handed it to Jacinta without tasting it. Then he again went off by himself. After thanking her godmother for the drinks, Jacinta and Lucia went in search of him. Finding him by the well, they asked why he didn't drink.

"When I took the glass," he answered, "I suddenly remembered I could offer that sacrifice to console Our Lord, so while you two were taking a drink, I ran over here." While Jacinta seemed always to be concerned with saving souls, these instances and others demonstrated Francisco's burning desire to console Our Lord.

One day after the first apparition of Our Lady, Francisco climbed to the top of a steep rock and called down that he wanted to stay there alone. Lucia and Jacinta went off to catch butterflies, but later they called up to him that it was lunchtime. He refused to eat and instead wanted to pray the rosary. Finally he called for the girls to join him. When they reached the top, Lucia asked what it was he had been doing. He replied, "I was thinking about God Who is so sad because of so many sins. If only I could give Him joy." Another day, after singing a little song, Francisco interrupted, "Let's not sing any more. Since we saw the angel and Our Lady, singing doesn't appeal to me any longer."

Sometime after the visions, when visitors besieged the children and plied them with questions, they accepted the interruptions as a sacrifice and patiently endured the repetitious telling of what they had witnessed. But, for all their sacrifices and prayers, they were still children, and sometimes they could take no more. One day, Francisco saw several ladies coming toward them and ran to tell his sister and cousin. All three immediately climbed up a nearby fig tree. Since the ladies were wearing fashionable hats with large brims, the children thought they would not be detected . . . and they were right.

Lucia relates that, as soon as the ladies left, "We came down as fast as we could, took to our heels, and hid in a cornfield."

Another time, Francisco avoided a crowd by climbing into the attic of his home where he could peer down and see everything. Later he explained to Lucia, "There were so many people! Heaven help me if they had ever caught me by myself. Whatever would I have said to them?"

Before he became ill — almost at the same time as Jacinta, in October 1918 —Francisco told Lucia, "Listen. You go to school, and I'll stay here in the church, close to the Hidden Jesus. Its not worth my while learning to read as I'll be going to heaven very soon. On your way home, come here and call me."

That was exactly where Lucia found him at the close of the school day. He was on his knees fervently praying. When he became ill, he often asked Lucia to visit the church for him and give his love to the Hidden Jesus. "What hurts me most is that I cannot go there myself and stay awhile."

During his illness, he suffered patiently, accepting everything offered to him so that his mother could not tell what he liked or disliked, what brought him comfort or discomfort. He is said never to have moaned or complained about the pain, but tried at all times to disguise what he was suffering. When asked by Lucia if he was suffering a great deal, he replied, "Yes, but I suffer it all for love of Our Lord and Our Lady."

Some months earlier, Lucia had found a length of rope in the street that she thought would be a good instrument of penance if worn around the waist. Jacinta and Francisco agreed, and all three then began wearing the rope in sacrifice for sinners. Only during his illness did Francisco finally give up the rope. He returned it to Lucia, saying, "Take it away before my mother sees it. I don't feel able to wear it any more around my waist." It seems his mother never knew that he was wearing this instrument of penance. Nor did their mother know that Jacinta also wore a piece of rope.

During Jacinta's illness she, like Francisco, surrendered her piece of rope to Lucia, who tells us, "Jacinta's cord had three knots, and was somewhat stained with blood. I kept it hidden until I finally left my mother's home. Then, not knowing what to do with it, I burned it, and Francisco's as well."

Children as well as adults came in great numbers to visit Francisco, with many remaining for long periods of time. He answered questions in as few words as possible and was patient and pleasant with everyone. Many remarked that they felt different in his presence, almost like one feels when in church.

In due time, Francisco confessed to his parish priest in preparation for his first Holy Communion. The next day, when he received the "Hidden Jesus," he was radiant with joy and said to his sister: "I am happier than you are, because I have the Hidden Jesus within my heart. I'm going to heaven, but I'm going to pray very much to Our Lord and Our Lady for them to bring you both there soon."

The day before his death, both Jacinta and Lucia spent the whole day with him. Because of his weakness he could not recite the rosary with them as he had before, so he asked them to pray the rosary for him instead. That night, Lucia said goodbye through her tears, in a heartfelt scene so intense Francisco's mother interrupted it. Francisco died of pneumonia the next day, April 4, 1919, ten months before his sister. At his death, he was ten years and ten months of age.

It is said that his face was illuminated in an angelic smile as, without any agony or contraction, he gently passed away. In the parochial enquiry, his mother declared, "His face lit up in a smile as he drew his last breath." His father agreed, adding, "He died smiling."

The Cause for the Beatification of the two little shepherds was introduced in 1952. Before the Cause could continue, the Plenary Assembly of the Congregation for the Causes of the Saints had to consider whether it was possible for small children who had not suffered martyrdom to practice virtue to a heroic degree. Finally, on April 2, 1981, the answer came back: yes, it was possible. Pope John Paul II approved the decision and conferred on the two little shepherds the title of Venerable on May 13, 1989.

The miracle required for their beatification involved a Portuguese woman, Maria Emilia Santos, bedridden in pain and unable to move from 1946 until 1989. Her cure was accepted on June 28, 1999, as having been "complete, enduring, and scientifically inexplicable."

In the presence of a tearful Lucia (Sr. Lucia of the Immaculate Heart), Pope John Paul II beatified Francisco and Jacinta Marto on May 13, 2000, in Fátima, Portugal. Jacinta is the youngest non-martyr to be beatified in the history of the church, and Francisco is the second youngest. +

Servant of God Guido de Fontgalland

1913 – 1925
12 years old
FRANCE

*H*e was only twelve years old when he died, but this young boy displayed a sanctity far beyond his years, nourished and encouraged by his deeply devout parents.

He was born on December 30, 1913, in Paris, where he attended school and received a good religious formation. But the real starting point of his rapid rise in sanctity was the reception of his first Holy Communion. He participated at the Holy Sacrifice of the Mass with unusual interest for one of his tender years and prepared for his first Holy Communion with the utmost affection and eagerness.

The grand event took place on May 22, 1921, when Jesus became present in his heart in an extraordinary manner. From then on Holy Mass was, for this small child, a source of joy and an occasion for the deepest contemplative prayer. He loved the Holy Mass with such intensity that his father once asked him how one should occupy himself during Mass. The young boy answered, "During Holy Mass our single occupation is to follow it thoughtfully. It is enough to read with the priest the prayers that he recites at the altar." But this youngster did more than just read the prayers; he seemed to relish the words of the priest and to love the object of the prayers with a great intensity.

Early in December 1924, Guido contracted diphtheria and knew instinctively that he would die. It was then that he turned to his mother and revealed the secret that he felt in his heart. He would die soon, but he lingered and endured without complaint all the ravages and crises of the disease.

Guido died on January 24, 1925, a month into his twelfth year.

His sanctity became so well known that a new school, when looking for a patron and a model of Christian life, chose him; the Congregation of the Barnabite Priests now conducts the Escuela Guido de Fontgalland. The goal of the school is the instruction and formation of children and the adolescent in a thoroughly Catholic atmosphere. So it is that this Parisian boy of twelve is the patron of a school in the Copacabana section of Rio De Janeiro, Brazil.

The Cause for Guido's Beatification was introduced in 1941. ✝

Servant of God Isabel Cristina Mrad Campos

1962 – 1982
19 years old
BRAZIL

The history of this nineteen-year-old martyr of purity ended in the town of Juiz de Fora, when she defended her virginity against a brutal attacker. But her brief life began happily when she was born on July 29, 1962, in Barbacena, Brazil.

She lived with her parents, José and Helena Campos, and an older brother, José Roberto, while she attended primary and secondary school. By the time she was ready for college, she had decided to study medicine.

Her first college housing was an apartment with a cousin and two friends, but this proved to be too crowded, so she moved into her brother's apartment. They decided that various alterations had to be made to the apartment and hired a carpenter. He began work right away — but also began to make obscene comments to Isabel in her brother's absence. Since he didn't finish the work in one day, he returned for a second day, discovered Isabel was alone, and was overcome by temptation. When he declared his intention, Isabel of course refused him, which enraged him. He threw her to the floor, tied her with ropes and belts, gagged her with pieces of fabric, and tore off her clothes. To muffle the sounds of the attack, he increased the volume of the radio and television; Isabel still resisted with all her strength. This so infuriated the man that he produced a knife and stabbed her fifteen times.

After her death, the Ecclesiastical Court took notice and prepared the preliminary steps toward Isabel's beatification. This was not only because of the manner of her death, but the purity of her life; an autopsy revealed that her virginity had been maintained.

In all respects, Isabel was an ordinary girl — she had a boyfriend, and attended the festivals and parties of her region — but she was extraordinary in the practice of her religion. She regularly attended Holy Mass and received the sacraments. Strengthened with the graces she received, she helped the needy. In school, she was always attentive to the girls who were poor, since their classmates did not always recognize their needs. She joined her parents and brother in a movement known as Vincentian Conferences, in which they played with poor children, fed the elderly, and did other acts of mercy. She also attended meetings of the Conference of St. Monica, to which her mother belonged.

After studying Isabel's virtuous and exemplary life, Archbishop of Mariana, Dom Luciano Mendes de Almeida, and other church authorities deemed her worthy of beatification and imitation. The process was opened in the city of her birth, to the edification and gratification of all who had known her. ✝

Blessed Isidore Bakanja

c. 1890 – 1904
14 years old
AFRICA

*W*hen various Belgian companies took possession of the Congo around the year 1885, they intended to enrich both their government and themselves by dealing in the country's riches of rubber and ivory, but the way they exploited the Congo's wealth entailed barbarous cruelty to the natives.

Belgian King Leopold II petitioned Pope Leo XIII to send missionaries who, it was hoped, would help ease the inhumane treatment of the workers. The pope responded by sending them the Trappists of Westmalle, Belgium, who arrived in 1895 and began their work in the central area of the Congo. These Trappists had much to do in helping the sick and instructing the illiterate natives; unfortunately, they had little effect on how the workers were treated. They managed to have the colonists' misconduct denounced by the Belgian government — but mere denouncements in a faraway country were no deterrent to the colonists and their personal drive for wealth. Thus, abuses continued largely with impunity, even after the missionaries arrived.

Isidore Bakanja was born around the time the Belgians arrived. In his early teens, he traveled down the river to the town of Mbandaka, where he obtained work as an assistant mason in the construction of buildings for the Belgian colonizers. It was in this town that Isidore met the missionary Fathers Gregoire Van Dun and Robert Brepols, who baptized him and trained him as a catechist. At his baptism, his name was inscribed in the baptismal registry and in the registry of the Scapular Confraternity.

The missionaries taught Isidore that a uniform identifies the profession of the person wearing it. Recognizing the natives' need for symbols, they stressed two devotions dear to Catholics: the rosary and the scapular. These would be the "uniform" by which their newfound treasure of faith would be recognized. Isidore viewed these symbols with deep affection and would not be parted from them, wearing them regardless of the sacrifice.

Several people who knew Isidore at this time testified, "He was of a very kindly nature. There were no arguments and he was a very good Christian." Another said, "Father, I could not find any evil in Isidore. We lived together. I was with my wife; as for him, he occupied the other side of the house. He was unmarried and never — absolutely never — did I hear that he had touched a woman. He was affable with everyone, black or white; never any arguments, and he prayed very much."

He returned to his native village and his Boangi tribe and began to build a house for himself, using the skills he had learned as a mason's helper. It is thought that he was contemplating marriage, but he soon became concerned that the Catholic faith had not as yet been preached in his region and began to instruct all who would listen to him. He abandoned construction and journeyed to Busira-Lokumo to live with a nephew, Camille Boyna. In this area, ceded to a Belgian company, he found work as a servant boy. But when his employer was transferred to a plantation in Ikili, Isidore was warned not to go. A fellow servant named Boyoto explained that the white people did not like people from downstream, and particularly did not like Christians.

Isidore, however, trusted his employer and accompanied him. Unfortunately, he soon learned that Boyoto's warnings were very true. On the Ikili plantation there was an anti-Christian freethinker by the name of Van Cauter (also known as Longange). He frequently made it known that Europe had rid itself of stupid priests and their false religion long ago.

Isidore's confidante at this time was a servant boy named Joseph Iyongo, who knew that Isidore experienced many difficulties. Soon after his arrival at the plantation, Longange demanded that Isidore stop teaching the natives how to pray. Isidore confided to Joseph Iyongo that he would pray while walking, or when alone in the house and added, "One time I had taken my rosary out of my pocket to go and pray while walking and the white man saw me and said, 'I don't want to see that contraption here. Go hide it in your box; you're here to work and not to mumble prayers.'"

When Isidore realized how much Longange hated him, he asked his employers for a letter releasing him so that he could return to his village. But Longange refused, sarcastically replying that he should ask his God for the letter.

So Isidore continued with his work and, during his free time, began to secretly instruct his fellow workers and the villagers about prayer and the beliefs of the Catholic faith.

One day when Isidore and his friend, Joseph Iyongo, were serving their masters supper, Longange saw the scapular around Isidore's neck and demanded that he take it off, saying that he never wanted to see "that thing" again. A few days later, Longange again noticed Isidore's scapular and flew into a rage. He ordered Isidore beaten with 25 strokes. Despite the beating, though, Isidore steadfastly refused to discard his scapular and rosary and continued his catechetical work.

A few days later, on February 2, 1909, while Longange was taking his afternoon coffee on the veranda, he saw Isidore walking toward the marsh saying his prayers and sent the servant boy, Iseboya, after him. The testimony of the servant boy reveals that when Isidore reported to Longange, he was told, "I'm fed up with your tricks. If you continue to instruct the people, my men will believe your lies. They'll want baptism, and then no one will want to work. All those things you teach them — like prayers you get from the stupid priests — they're nothing but lies! Lie down for a whipping."

Isidore countered, "But why, white man? I stole nothing of yours . . . I never went near your wife. . . . Why do you want to beat me?"

Furious, Longange shouted, "Shut up, animal of stupid priests. I'm thrashing you because you are teaching the stupid priests' prayers and all sorts of stupidities to my workers, to my servant boys and even to the villagers . . ."

On the veranda was a whip made of elephant hide that had been damaged during construction. Longange had repaired it with two nails at one end that protruded through the hide. Grabbing his new whip, he called his head domestic, Bongele, and ordered him to beat Isidore. Bongele resisted because of the two nails at the end, but Longange threatened his life if he continued to protest.

First, Longange ripped the scapular from Isidore's neck and threw it to the dogs, who ran off with it. Then, taking Isidore by the neck, he threw the boy to the ground and ordered the beating to commence. Bongele began the lashing, holding the end of the strap with the two nails in his hand — but that wasn't good enough for Longange. He demanded that Isidore should be beaten with the nail end of the whip, and harder. He again threatened the death of both servants if the beating was not to his liking.

Afraid for his life, the servant obeyed, and two other servant boys came in to assist; one held Isidore's hands, the other his feet. When Isidore writhed in pain, Longange pressed his foot on his shoulders and kicked him repeatedly. Finally, Isidore pleaded for mercy, telling Longange that he was dying. Longange responded by pressing the boy's head into the dirt and ordering him to be quiet. The beating stopped only when Bongele could no longer continue because of fatigue. It was estimated that Isidore sustained 200 to 250 blows, the majority on his back.

Isidore attempted to rise from his pool of blood murmuring, "The white man has killed me with his whip. . . . He did not want me to pray to God. . . . He killed me because I said my prayers . . . . I stole nothing from him. . . . It's because I was praying to God."

Hoping Isidore would die in isolation so that his death would not be reported to the authorities, Longange had Isidore chained by the feet in the room where rubber was processed. This began Isidore's Calvary: deposited on a dirty mat in a filthy room, he was at the mercy of mosquitoes and other insects that tormented his already infected wounds. A bowl of rice and another of water were left near him, but he lacked the strength to feed himself. Additionally, the dense odors of burning rubber made him cough, adding to his misery.

Finally, several days later, the company's inspector came for a visit. Horrified at what he saw, the inspector called Longange to the scene. When Isidore explained that he did nothing wrong, Longange became enraged, slapped Isidore in the face, and ordered that he be killed. The inspector, however, barred his way and warned Longange that he would be reported to the Belgian authorities. The court later condemned Longange.

The inspector had Isidore brought to his boat, where he personally tended the wounds. Later he left Isidore at a plantation known as Ngomb Isongu, where the company provided food and medication for him. A young servant boy remembers, "I slept near him, Isidore on the bed and I by the fire in front of the bed. Isidore had been atrociously wounded, but he never abandoned his prayers. He prayed very much. . . ." In spite of his wounds, Isidore continue his catechetical work as young villagers gathered around him and marveled how a man who had been so abused could still pray to his God. Many villagers later received Baptism after witnessing Isidore's acceptance of suffering and his longing for heaven.

Eventually, Isidore was brought to the home of his nephew who found that caring for the seriously injured young man was too much for him. Isidore was then entrusted to Bolangi, who lived in front of the catechist Loleka. While there, Father Gregoire heard Isidore's confession and gave him the Anointing of the Sick on July 24, 1909. The next day, Isidore received the Holy Eucharist, much to his joy and consolation. When asked by the priest the cause of the beating, Isidore explained his innocence: "The white man did not like Christians.... He did not want me to wear the scapular.... He yelled at me when I said my prayers."

Fr. Gregoire stayed several days with Isidore, offering him some consoling thoughts, but Isidore always answered: "It's nothing if I die. If God wants me to live, I'll live! If God wants me to die, I'll die. It's all the same to me." When the priest urged forgiveness, Isidore replied, "I'm not angry with the white man. He beat me. That's his business; it is none of mine. He should know what he is doing.... I shall pray for him when I am in heaven. I shall pray for him very much."

Once again, the care of Isidore was too much. Isidore then spent the rest of his days on the porch of the catechist. His wounds were dressed with medicines provided by the director of the Belgian company, but the wounds were too infected to hope for healing. In time, Isidore's entire body became infected, with his hips and bones protruding through his skin. His neck also caused atrocious pain from the kicks he had received from Longange the day of his beating. All through this ordeal, Isidore was seen with his rosary and was often seen praying it.

Eventually on Sunday, August 8 or 15, Isidore began vomiting blood and decaying matter. Then somehow, with everyone expecting him to die at any moment, he gathered enough strength to stand up and walk into a nearby banana patch to pray, something he had often done before the beating. After a time, with his rosary in his hand, he walked back and returned to his mat. All the witnesses wondered how he could have managed to do such a thing because of his severe weakness, having been unable to stand or sit. Since his beating, he was forced to lie on his stomach because of his festering wounds, with every movement causing unbearable pain.

Isidore then participated in the Sunday prayer session held by the Catholics in the catechist's home. He ate a simple meal provided by

Maria Saola, then died shortly thereafter. He was buried during a simple service with a scapular around his neck and a rosary in his hands. Attending the funeral was a large number of Catholics and non-Christians who mourned the death of their holy countryman.

The Congo, now known as Zaire, won its independence from Belgium in 1960. When Pope John Paul II visited Zaire in May of 1980, he praised Isidore Bakanja, saying:

> I speak of a Zairois catechist, Isidore Bakanja, a true Zairois, a true Christian. After having given all his free time to the evangelization of his brothers as a catechist, he did not hesitate to offer his life to God, strong in the courage he found in his faith and in the faithful recitation of the rosary.

Since Isidore had been enrolled as a member of the Scapular Confraternity at the time of his baptism, a fact noted in the registry of the parish confraternity, the General Council of the Carmelite Order in 1984 declared that Isidore was, "a gift from God and from the Blessed Virgin Mary. The scapular devotion has its martyr."

Pope John Paul II beatified Isidore on April 24, 1994. +

Blessed Jacinta Marto

1910 – 1920
9 years 11 months
PORTUGAL

*I*n her memoirs, Lucia dos Santos (Sr. Mary Lucia of the Immaculate Heart) wrote: "Before the visions of 1916-1917, apart from the ties of relationship that united us, no other particular affection led me to prefer the companionship of Jacinta and Francisco to that of any other child."

Why was this? Francisco, for his part, was a very quiet lad, but "Jacinta's company I found to be very disagreeable on account of her oversensitive temperament."

Lucia tells us that Jacinta would pout and run off by herself at the slightest disagreement during a game when it was not going as she wanted, and no amount of coaxing from the other children could entice her to return. She insisted on choosing her partner for all games, as well as choosing which game they would play. But, Lucia adds, God endowed Jacinta with a sweet and gentle character, making her at once lovable and attractive. In short, Jacinta was the personification of enthusiasm and caprice, even before the apparitions.

After the apparitions, Lucia tells us, "Jacinta's demeanor was always serious and reserved, but friendly. All her actions seemed to reflect the presence of God in the way proper to people of mature age and great virtue." After her death, Jacinta's father added that she "was the sweetest among our children."

So although Lucia did not choose Jacinta and her brother, Francisco, for companions, they invariably chose her. They would persuade Lucia to join them at the well at the bottom of the garden belonging to Lucia's parents. Once there, Jacinta chose the game to be played, her favorites being Pebbles and Buttons, which they played in the shade of olive and plum trees. The game Buttons consisted of snapping off the buttons of the loser. This, we are told, left Lucia often in a predicament, since Jacinta usually won them all and refused to give them back until Lucia threatened not to play with her again.

Sometimes, when her mother told Lucia to stay near the house, the children played there until siesta time. Then, Lucia's mother conducted Catechism lessons, which Jacinta and Francisco attended.

One of the activities Jacinta loved the most was sitting outside in the evenings with Lucia and Francisco. They contemplated the beautiful sunsets and tried to count the stars. They called the stars "angels' lamps," the moon "Our Lady's lamp," and the sun "Our Lord's lamp." Jacinta preferred the moon, since "it doesn't burn us up or blind us the way Our Lord's does." It is known that Jacinta suffered greatly from the heat.

When Jacinta expressed a desire to receive Holy Communion as Lucia was doing, it was explained that Lucia was older at ten years, the usual age for the first reception of the Eucharist, and that Jacinta did not yet know her Catechism. Since both Jacinta and Francisco wanted to receive "the Hidden Jesus," Lucia began to teach them, an easy assignment since both were attentive and enthusiastic students. Although Jacinta did not receive her first Holy Communion in the normal manner, during the apparition of the angel, both she and Francisco drank from the chalice after Lucia had received the Host. Jacinta also benefited from making frequent spiritual communions of desire.

When Lucia began to tend the family's sheep, the two children were at first denied permission to go with her, but they waited for her return and joined her at the threshing floor, where they awaited the light from Our Lady's lamp and those of the angels. But eventually, Jacinta and Francisco began to tend their family's sheep with those of Lucia. While the sheep grazed, the children climbed to the top of a hill and shouted names that echoed back to them. Jacinta sometimes said the whole Hail Mary that way, echoing each word in its turn. They sang songs familiar to children, but also religious ones, which they sang with reverence. Jacinta loved dancing; the slightest melody played by a faraway shepherd set her feet to moving and her little body to swaying.

The children were told by their parents to say a rosary after eating their lunch, but they theorized they would have more time for play if they abbreviated the prayers to just two words each. So it was that they passed the beads through their fingers while saying, "Hail Mary. Hail Mary," on occasion, causing the words to echo through the hills. At the end of each decade, they also shortened the Our Father to the two words, "Our Father." Satisfied they had been obedient to what was asked of them, they went off happily for more games.

Lucia noticed that Jacinta loved to hold little white lambs, kissing them and carrying them home on her shoulders so that they wouldn't get tired. One day, when Jacinta walked in the midst of the flock while going home, Lucia asked the reason for her choosing to carry the lambs. It turned out Jacinta was re-enacting the scene from a holy card in which Our Lord was depicted as the Good Shepherd.

Since the apparitions of the angel and those of our Blessed Mother at the Cova de Iria are so well known, we will not relate them here. Suffice to say after the vision in which the children saw hell, Jacinta was so impressed that she could not understand the concept of it as never ending and would often stop their games to ask Lucia about it. More than this, Jacinta was so deeply concerned that she resolved to make many sacrifices to save sinners from such a terrifying eternity. It truly was this vision that prompted the three little shepherd children to make great spiritual progress.

Jacinta is said never to have missed an opportunity to make a sacrifice. Giving up their lunches became their usual sacrifice. Beggar children were the happy recipients of these lunches, but when the little beggars could not be found, the three children fed their lunches to the sheep. Instead of the nice food that had been prepared for them, they ate acorns, choosing the bitterest ones as a sacrifice. Other times they ate pine nuts, blackberries, mushrooms, or whatever they could find along the way.

Another favorite sacrifice was to endure thirst, especially hard during the heat of summer. On some occasions they were given clusters of grapes, which Jacinta gave to the poor children playing on the road. Another time she had figs and was about to eat them, then hesitated and put them back in the basket, offering them in sacrifice. Lucia writes, "Jacinta made such sacrifices over and over again, but I won't stop to tell any more, or I shall never end."

Jacinta is said to have had a vision of people throwing stones at the Holy Father. After the apparitions, when two priests questioned the children, the priests recommended that they pray for the Holy Father. After the priests explained who the Holy Father was, Jacinta developed such a love for the Pope that every time she offered her sacrifices to Jesus she added, "and for the Holy Father." She often prayed for him and always added three Hail Marys for him after the recitation of the Rosary.

When pilgrims who wanted to see them besieged the little village, the children found countless opportunities for sacrifices. Having to repeat over and over the events they had witnessed, the children grew weary. Still, they obliged these requests, always making the sacrifice for love of Jesus and the Immaculate Heart of Mary, and for the conversion of sinners.

Lucia also reports that people were always asking questions or telling the children about their needs and troubles. Jacinta showed the greatest compassion to these people, but sometimes, the children felt the need to hide. This they would do in a cave located on the eastern side of a hill, where they were sheltered from the sun by oak and olive trees. There they offered countless rosaries.

When the children were sent to prison, this too was offered as a sacrifice for sinners — but when they were told they would be "fried alive" for not revealing to the Administrator the secret confided to them by the Lady, Jacinta began to cry. The tears were not in fright of her impending doom, but because she wanted to see her mother one last time. When asked if she wanted to offer this sacrifice for the conversion of sinners, she acknowledged that she did. She then folded her hands in prayer, and through her tears she recited the familiar prayer, "O my Jesus! This is for love of You, for the conversion of sinners, for the Holy Father, and in reparation for the sins committed against the Immaculate Heart of Mary."

When one of the prisoners suggested that all could be avoided if they revealed the secret, Jacinta replied enthusiastically, "Never! I would rather die." She literally believed the threat of the Administrator that they would be "fried alive" if they did not reveal the secret given by the Lady, so this was truly a heroic declaration.

In addition to her many sacrifices Jacinta often said ejaculations. One day, when she was ill, she told Lucia, "I so like to tell Jesus that I love Him! Many times, when I say it to Him, I seem to have a fire in my heart, but it doesn't burn me. I love Our Lord and Our Lady so much, that I never get tired of telling them that I love them."

What one might consider small miracles were attributed to Jacinta's prayers. A poor woman was afflicted with a terrible disease, but when she saw Jacinta on the road, she knelt before the child and begged her to ask Our Lady for a cure. The woman would not rise, and Jacinta felt uneasy with the woman kneeling before her, so Jacinta also knelt down and recited three Hail Marys with the woman. When they both rose to their feet, Jacinta assured her that Our Lady would cure her, and that she would continue to pray for her. Sometime later the poor woman returned to thank Our Lady.

Another time, a soldier who had been called to the front wept bitterly because he would be forced to leave his sick wife with their three small children. Jacinta tried to comfort him by saying, "Don't cry. Our Lady is so good! She will certainly grant you the grace you are asking." She continued to pray for the soldier who, some time later, returned with his wife and his children, Our Lady had afforded the family two graces: the soldier was released from service after contracting a fever on the eve of his departure, and the wife attributed her cure to the Blessed Virgin.

Jacinta's sacrifices continued even after she contracted influenza, then suffered from various complications that would eventually claim her life. At first, she declined water when she was thirsty, but she soon realized that she could make many sacrifices by obediently drinking water, broth, or milk, or whatever was offered to her. This she did enthusiastically and without complaint.

One day when Lucia visited the two very ill patients, Jacinta announced, "Our Lady came to see us. She told us she would come to take Francisco to heaven very soon, and she asked me if I still wanted to convert more sinners. I said I did. She told me I would be going to a hospital where I would suffer for the conversion of sinners...."

When Francisco appeared to be dying, Jacinta confided to him, "Give all my love to Our Lord and Our Lady, and tell them that I'll suffer as much as they want for the conversion of sinners and in reparation to the Immaculate Heart of Mary." After a hospital stay, Jacinta returned home for a short time. She had a large open wound in her chest that had to be treated every day, but she endured all without complaint and without the least sign of irritation. Even while in this condition, she was besieged by visitors who questioned her about the visions — all this she endured for her usual intentions.

Once again, Our Lady visited her. Jacinta told Lucia, "She told me that I am going to Lisbon to another hospital; that I will not see you again, nor my parents either, and after suffering a great deal, I shall die alone. But she said I must not be afraid, since she herself is coming to take me to heaven." She cried after repeating this to Lucia saying, "I shall never see you again! Please pray hard for me, since I am going to die alone," When Lucia told her not to think about it, Jacinta replied, "Let me think about it since the more I think, the more I suffer, and I want to suffer for love of Our Lord for sinners."

One day when Lucia was speaking with Jacinta's mother, Jacinta called Lucia to her bedside with the request, "I don't want you to tell anybody that I'm suffering, not even my mother. I do not want to upset her."

The day Jacinta left home for Lisbon was one with tears shed on all sides, and with promises of prayers. One can only imagine the sadness of that day. Soon, Jacinta sent word from the hospital that Our Lady had visited her again, telling her the exact day and hour of her death. (She, in fact, died one month later on February 20, 1920, at 10:30 p.m., only ten months after the death of Francisco.) But prior to her death, at the hospital in Lisbon, her doctor spoke of how she had endured pain and suffering during an operation in which inflamed tissue was removed with only local anesthesia. The doctor exclaimed, "I got the impression that this child had great courage. The only words I heard her say during the operation were: 'Oh my Jesus! Oh my God!'" The doctor added that Jacinta's patience was "absolutely heroic."

Lucia asked: "How is it that Jacinta, small as she was, let herself be driven by such a spirit of mortification and penance, and understood it so well?" Then, she answered her own question: "I think the reason is this: firstly, God willed to bestow on her a special grace through the Immaculate Heart of Mary; and secondly, it was because she had looked upon hell and had seen the ruin of souls who fall therein." Finally she added, "I think Jacinta was the one who received from Our Lady a greater abundance of grace, and a better knowledge of God and of virtue."

Pope John Paul II recognized this holiness when he beatified the little brother and sister on May 13, 2000, the anniversary of the first vision; it was also the anniversary of the attempt on the pope's life that had taken place on May 13, 1981.

During the Beatification ceremony, attended by more than half a million people, the pope said:

As at Lourdes, the Virgin in Fátima chose children to be the recipients of her message. They accepted it so faithfully, not only meriting recognition as credible witnesses of the apparitions, but also by becoming themselves examples of living the Gospel.

The pope also made it clear that they were not being beatified simply because they received the apparitions, but because "even though they were not martyrs, they demonstrated lives of Christian virtue of heroic proportions, in spite of their tender age. It was the heroism of children, but it was true heroism."

Attending the beatification ceremony was Lucia, then Sr. Mary Lucia of the Immaculate Heart, a Discalced Carmelite nun. At 93 years of age, she met twice with the pope on that visit, his third visit to Fátima.

During the process that brought the children to their beatification, the recognition of their remains had to be performed. The first exhumation took place on September 12, 1935. Jacinta's father, after looking at his daughter's body, remarked that it "was somewhat like looking at a person grown old, whom one had known young." The father's description was echoed by others, who also thought Jacinta's face appeared much older than she was at the time of her death. Some thought the reason was that her features reflected her spiritual maturity. When the coverings were folded back, revealing only the upper portion of the body, it was discovered that Jacinta's body had remained incorrupt. Official observers noted that, while natural explanations could he given for incorruption in some cases, in the case of Jacinta it seemed to be supernatural — because at the time of her burial, it was not customary for bodies in Portugal to be embalmed.

The body was exhumed a second time on April 30, 1951, and on May 5 of that same year, the little shepherdess was buried in a tomb next to that of her brother in the Basilica. Here, countless pilgrims visit the two little Blesseds.

Jacinta was only nine years and eleven months old at the time of her death, and Francisco was eleven years and ten months old. They are the youngest children ever to be beatified without dying martyrs' deaths. +

Servant of God José Sánchez del Rio

1913 – 1928
15 years old
MEXICO

*J*osé's wealthy and pious family provided him with the luxuries of life and a deep appreciation and love of the Church. He was born in Sahuayo, in the district of Michoacan on March 28, 1913. He was known as a handsome lad, pleasant, restless, and mischievous, but very obedient and affectionate with his parents. He attended primary school and received his first Holy Communion at the age of nine. Even at this tender age, he often received the sacraments and prayed the rosary with great attention and pleasure.

Some years later, when the government began its persecution against the Catholic Church, José was sent to Guadalajara in the neighboring state of Jalisco, where he attended school until 1926. Here, he and his older brother (like so many other young saints) joined Catholic Action, to help the Church by helping the poor and the sick.

When José was thirteen, the persecution intensified, prompting him to join the Cristero movement in opposition to his family's wishes. (It was during this persecution that Blessed Miguel Pro, in disguise, performed his priestly and charitable duties for the people of the underground Catholic Church.) Inflamed with the desire to fight for the rights of the Catholic Church despite his tender age, José took up weapons prepared to fight and die for the kingdom of God. Catholic men of all ages determined to resist the persecution were amused at the youngster's fervor and nicknamed him "Tarcisio" in honor of the third-century Roman martyr, Tarcisius, who died in defense of the Holy Eucharist.

After fighting for two years beside much older men, José was captured and taken prisoner. Together with an Indian boy, he was brought to Sahuayo to be judged as a criminal of the state with the definite possibility of execution. From his prison cell, he wrote a poignant letter to his mother in which he told her of his imprisonment. Dated February 6, 1928, the letter reads, in part:

> I am resigned to the will of God. I die very happy because I die beside Our Lord. Do not afflict yourself because of my death since to die for God gives me joy. I send greetings to my brothers and ask them to always follow the smallest wish of God. I ask you to send me your blessing together with that of my father. I greet all for the last time. I send you love from your child's heart and desire so much to see you before dying. . . .

José was held prisoner with his companion for some days in the baptistery of the parish church of St. John, but was given several opportunities to escape. Without hesitation, he refused and pleaded with his father not to pay the ransom for his release, since he was offering his life to God. Toward the evening of February 10, José's companion, the small Indian boy, was brought outside and hanged on a tree in the main plaza of the city; however, this attempt at execution failed, and he was discovered to be still alive when brought to the cemetery. He was fully revived and, in a surprising act of kindness, the cemetery workers — not knowing what else to do with him — allowed him to run away in the dark.

All during his imprisonment, José had faithfully recited his rosary and sung sacred songs, anticipating his desired martyrdom. Soon after the unsuccessful hanging of his Indian companion, the government soldiers, apparently unwilling to let the people see them executing a small boy, took José outside under cover of night. When he began to shout *"Viva Cristo Rey!"* ("Long live Christ the King!"), the shout of the revolutionaries, the soldiers became so infuriated that they first tried to suffocate him. When this was unsuccessful and he again shouted his love of God, they stabbed him. But the official on the scene finally ordered that he be killed with a fierce blow to the head with the butt of a gun. Another report tells that the boy was also shot in the head.

Today, the remains of the little martyr who had fought for the rights of the Church rest in an underground crypt in the Church of the Sacred Heart of Jesus, together with the remains of 27 fellow soldiers, killed a little later.

His process of beatification, initiated in 1996 by the Bishop of Zamora, Mexico, has been under the examination of the Congregation of the Causes of the Saints since February 8, 1999. ✝

Servant of God Joseph (Peppino) Ottone

1928 – 1940
12 years old
ITALY

*J*oseph's life had a sad beginning: he was the product of an inces-
tuous relationship of a married woman. The husband, who had
immigrated to Argentina, refused to return when he learned of his
wife's unfaithfulness. She would have aborted the child had it not been
for the pleadings of a friend, who advised her to have the baby and
then offer it for adoption.

So it was that Joseph was born on March 18, 1928, in Castel-
pagano (Benevento) and was baptized in the Church of St. Salvatore.
His birth was registered the next day in the magistrate's office under
the name Giuseppe Italico.

Within a few days, he was delivered to the provincial hospital with
only the clothes he was wearing. He stayed there until November 22
of the same year, when Dominic and Maria Ottone applied for his
adoption. Unable to have children of their own, the couple was
delighted to have this child to raise with love and tenderness.

The couple soon moved with Joseph from Benevento to Torre
Annunziata, a small town near Naples. Surprisingly, the natural mother

kept in touch with the adoptive parents and watched Joseph from a distance for many years, being very pleased with his progress in his studies and in his advance in virtue. She died in 1955 and, knowing what a kind and remarkable child she had borne, called herself *indegna madre,* "unworthy mother."

Whether or not Joseph knew his natural mother, or whether the natural mother knew of the real conditions of the Ottone household, is unknown. Joseph's adoptive mother was a religious woman, of a good nature, peaceful and kind, who dearly loved him. Such was not the case with his adoptive father, however. That man was cruel, disagreeable, argumentative, and frequently intoxicated. When difficulties arose, Joseph was an angel of peace, trying to always protect Maria Ottone and restore tranquility to the household.

In spite of trouble at home, Joseph grew into a fine youngster with many virtues. He had started his studies at the local school in 1934 and went gladly, never seeming dissatisfied with his studies. Studious and friendly to all, he was very attracted to the practice of his faith. He received his first Holy Communion on May 26, 1935; on the same day he was admitted to the Archconfraternity of the Holy Rosary. From then on, he increased in virtue with the determination of a saint, assiduously praying and faithfully observing First Fridays and First Saturdays. He is known to have often traveled on his bicycle to nearby Pompeii to visit the magnificent sanctuary of the Holy Rosary, founded by Blessed Bartolo Longo. Closer to home, he stopped every morning in the parish church for a brief visit to the Holy Eucharist before attending school, even though his friends often teased him about it.

Although he was given to prayer far more than boys his own age, he nevertheless was a normal boy who studied hard, played games with his friends, and had dreams like others — particularly the dream of being a great mariner. Most boys his age also had this ambition, being inspired by the many magnificent ships that docked in the Gulf of Naples.

Joseph continued studying at the local school from 1934 until 1939, when he transferred to the Istituto Tecnico Commerciale; there, he again excelled in his studies.

When Joseph was twelve years old, his adopted mother became seriously ill and required an operation. Since this was unsuccessful a second operation was needed. On February 3, 1940, Joseph was extremely concerned about his dear mother, and was walking with friends near the hospital when he looked down and found on the ground a small image of the Madonna of Pompeii. He picked it up, kissed it, and asked his heavenly Mother if he could exchange his life for that of his adopted mother. It is reported that he immediately became pale and fainted. At the hospital he was unconscious, with a weak pulse and rapid respiration. His prayer was answered when medical remedies proved to be unsuccessful. He died the next day at only twelve years of age. After his brave sacrifice, his adoptive mother recovered and continued on in good health to her eighty-eighth year.

Church authorities soon became aware of the many people who honored Joseph's memory and began the process for his eventual beatification. He was regarded as a bright star of innocence, self-sacrifice, and virtue, which could well serve as a model for adolescent boys of our time.

The Congregation for the Causes of Saints made the last action on Joseph's case in 1982. ✝

Servant of God Josephina Vilaseca

1940 – 1952
12 years old
SPAIN

C he story of this little twelve-year-old is simply told.

She was born March 9, 1940, at Horta de Avino, Diocese of Vich, in the northeastern section of Spain. Her family was of humble and modest means, but honest and faithful Christian people.

Josephina recited the Holy Rosary every day and enrolled in the Association of the Daughters of Mary. She is known to have practiced penances, especially on the First Fridays and First Saturdays of each month, and to have an extraordinary love of the Blessed Mother. Her love of others found its outlet through her participation in the Catholic Action organization.

Although of tender years, she was placed in the service of a nearby family, where she performed her household duties with utmost care and diligence. While she was pleased with her new position, however, there was one disturbing element — a young man of the family took a fancy to her and tried on numerous occasions to win her with his amorous advances. She habitually repulsed them all until one day, when he laid a trap for her. Unable to escape, she fought valiantly with all her strength against his sinful desires. Finally, furious at her resistance, he mortally wounded her.

As she lay in the hospital in agonizing pain, she forgave her assailant and died on December 4, 1952; she may well be another St. Maria Goretti, having preferred death to offending God.

The Cause for Beatification of this victim of holy purity was begun in 1958. ✝

Blessed Laura Vicuña

1891 – 1904
13 years old
CHILE/ARGENTINA

A vicious civil war was in progress in Chile when Laura Vicuña was born, on April 5, 1891. Her father, José Domingo Vicuña, was a soldier who belonged to a noble Chilean family. When the conservative party was defeated, producing a period of struggle and anxiety, Señor Vicuña was forced to flee the country. During his exile, after much physical and mental suffering, Señor Vicuña died, leaving his wife, Señora Mercedes, a widow with two young daughters.

Realizing that she and the children could not survive at that time in Santiago, Chile, she crossed the Andes with them and settled in Argentina. Unfortunately, she was unable to find employment in a strange country, surrounded by moral and other dangers. Worried and anxious about their survival, she eventually found work at Quilquihue, a large hacienda owned by Señor Manuel Mora. Unfortunately, this was a bad choice — arrogant and quarrelsome, he fancied himself a great Latin lover.

The poor widow was in a precarious position, having little money and two girls to support. Señor Mora promised to help and protect her little family, and soon seduced her. Realizing that her situation was not a wholesome environment for her daughters, Laura and Julia, Señora Mercedes enrolled them as pupils in the Salesian school in Junin through the generosity of her benefactor.

Under the patronage of Mary, Help of Christians, the Salesian sisters provided a good scholastic and religious education, which Laura's eager mind happily absorbed.

Laura discovered God and blossomed in her love for Him and His Blessed Mother. As a result, she saw God in her companions and did all she could for them, doing various charitable deeds and maintaining peace as she settled squabbles. Laura was everyone's friend. She was a leader in sports and generously forgave little annoyances that developed.

Father Paul Aronica, in his biography of Laura, quotes a classmate as saying: "She loved the poor girls. If she had been free to do so, she would have given them all she had. She was pained if any one of us hurt a poor child by laughing at her clothes or her poverty. She would never let us poke fun at anyone and, while she was always kind, she became severe with us if we started being mean."

Sr. Angela, the superior of the school, reinforces this when she wrote: "Laura used to give those poor children whatever pennies her mother gave her. She would even give them some of her clothes, her playthings, sometimes her food. She used to cheer them up with her kindness."

Laura especially admired the sisters who had left their countries, homes, and relatives to dedicate themselves to others in a foreign land. She understood that with God so close to them, they were quick with their smiles, generous with all, and eager to share God with others. Laura soon harbored a secret desire to join them in religious life. After consulting with her spiritual director, Father Crestanello, she understood that since she was only eleven years old, it was impossible for her to take the formal vows of a Salesian sister. Nevertheless, she implored him to permit her to take private religious vows of poverty, chastity, and obedience. After much hesitation, but noting her deep sincerity and the spiritual state of her soul, he granted permission.

One day Sr. Rose was talking to her students about the sacrament of Matrimony. The children, especially Laura, instinctively realized her mother's situation. Dismayed that her mother was far away from God, and that Señor Mora was the reason, Laura decided to pray especially hard that her mother would discover the love of God and return to the sacraments. She is known to have often prayed before the Holy Eucharist, "I'll fight for my Mother even at the cost of my life.... yes, my life for hers." She was determined to save her mother's soul.

When the holidays approached, Laura was excited about visiting Quilquihue and enjoying her mother's loving care. She and Julia were overjoyed at the prospect, but Laura was also distressed because without a chapel nearby, she would be unable to visit the Holy Eucharist. All went well during the holidays except for a strange feeling she experienced in the presence of Señor Mora.

After returning to school, Laura could not forget her mother and her terrible situation and fully understood what was taking place.

Her first Holy Communion took place on the second of June, 1901. In her little notebook she wrote, "Oh my God, I want to love you and serve you all my life. . . . I give you my soul, my heart, my whole self."

From that day onward she resolved to love God with her whole heart and her whole strength. Her one aim was to say at the end of each day, "Today I have refused you nothing, dear Lord. . . . Give me a life of loving service, of mortification, of sacrifice." The Lord answered that prayer, for Laura's spiritual life continued to blossom. When she was enrolled in the Sodality of the Children of Mary, she received a medallion symbolizing her deep and tender love of the Blessed Virgin. She would wear it as a shield against spiritual dangers.

When the school year was completed, Laura and her sister returned to the hacienda. But once she was there, Señor Mora wasted no time in giving her unwanted attentions. Laura was deeply concerned and resorted to prayer, knowing full well that she would be tested. Once when she was alone with Señor Mora, he embraced her affectionately, but she managed to wiggle free, a rebuff that made him furious.

Sometime afterwards the two girls, their mother, and Señor Mora attended a lavish fiesta. In the evening's lively dancing, Señor Mora approached Laura and asked her to dance with him, but she refused. Señor Mora could no longer restrain his anger and began to threaten her. Seeing his emotional state, Señora Mercedes entreated Laura to dance, reminding her that it was not sinful to do so. Laura again refused and ran outside to hide in the dark. Señor Mora did not accept this second rejection kindly, but vented his anger on the mother. Afraid to venture out of her hiding place, Laura clasped the medal that symbolized her dedication as a Child of Mary and appealed to the Blessed Virgin for protection.

Amid threats of more violence, Señor Mora committed his ultimate act of revenge: he discontinued payment of the girls' school expenses. The sisters, on learning of this, decided to accept the girls without payment, but Señora Mercedes, embarrassed by this generosity, sent only Laura back for the next session.

Restored to the peace of the school and the influence of the sisters, Laura was once again happy, but her smile hid her concern for her mother, still at the mercy of Señora Mora's violent temper.

After her Confirmation on Easter Sunday 1902, she consulted her confessor, Fr. Crestanello, for permission to officially offer to sacrifice her life for her mother's. After a time, realizing that Laura fully knew the consequences, the priest gave his consent. Thus it was that she once again offered her life for the spiritual conversion of her mother.

The following year, Laura became ill due to the damp and rainy weather at the school. She became so weak that the sisters thought it best for her mother to take her home to Quilquihue, where the climate was pleasant. But Laura's condition continued to deteriorate, to the point that her mother rented a room in Junín instead, so that her daughter could be closer to a doctor and medical care. Although Laura's condition was serious, she often smiled knowingly at her mother — a smile Señora Mercedes could not interpret.

It was in mid-January of 1904 when Señor Mora decided to visit the cottage where Laura and her mother were staying. When he announced that he intended to spend the night there, Señora Mercedes tried to discourage him, but he refused to leave. Even though seriously weakened, Laura said resolutely, "If he stays, I will go." Without waiting for a reaction, she gathered what little strength she had left and walked outside. Furious at this third rejection, Señor Mora followed her outside and beat the girl until she collapsed.

After this fierce beating, Laura returned to her bed and never left it. Señora Mercedes remained day and night by her side, lavishing every care and attention on her suffering daughter. When Laura realized that she was close to death, she looked tenderly at her mother and revealed her secret. "Mother, I'm about to die, but I'm happy to offer my life for you. I asked Our Lord for this."

Humbled by this tremendous sacrifice, Señora Mercedes fell to her knees, sobbing. She asked forgiveness of the dying girl and promised that she would abandon her life of sin and return to the embrace of the Church.

Now happy that her prayer was answered, Laura Vicuña died on January 22, 1904. She was not yet thirteen years old. It can be truly stated that she died for the cause of purity much as St. Maria Goretti had died in defense of her purity only two years earlier.

Laura was buried in the local cemetery where, almost at once, the people of the town made her tomb a shrine with offerings of flowers and prayers. Then, in 1954, the Argentine government authorized the transfer of her remains to the grounds of the school operated by the Salesian sisters. Soon after this, the apostolic process was started that could lead to Laura's canonization.

Laura Vicuña is only one step away from realizing this status, as Pope John Paul II beatified her on September 3, 1988. ✝

Servant of God Lorena D'Alexander

1964 – 1981
16 years old
ITALY

The life of this Servant of God became so well known, with so many being edified by her virtues, that her memory is now entrusted to an organization known as *Associazione Amici di Lorena,* dedicated to advancing her Cause for Beatification.

Known as the Flower of the Parish, Lorena was born in La Rustica, a district on the outskirts of Rome, to a family of modest means. Her parents, Giovanni and Alba Avalle, were also blessed with a son, Tonino, and another girl, Simona.

Lorena was a happy, keenly intelligent child, but of a delicate nature. At the age of ten, she had operations for tonsillitis and appendicitis. She recovered completely in time to receive her first Holy Communion in May 1974. Sickness seemed to be her vocation, however, since the following September, a tumor was discovered in her left leg. Doctors operated immediately to remove the tumor and replace it with bone taken from another region of her body. After a time Lorena was able to walk again, although with great difficulty. But she returned to school undaunted, and excelled in literary studies, proving to be an accomplished poet.

Soon after receiving the sacrament of Confirmation in 1976, Lorena had trouble with her leg once more. The tumor had returned; the only means left to save her life was to amputate her leg. The doctors consulted with the worried parents, who gave permission for the operation. Lorena was to write later, "I am happy that my parents chose life for me."

Lorena was courageous in accepting the decision, cooperated cheerfully with all the preoperative tests and postoperative remedies, and reassured her parents that all would be well. The operation was a success and in no time at all, Lorena was able to travel about the hospital in a wheelchair. Her greatest pleasure was visiting the other patients, helping them as much as she could, and telling them little stories to entertain them. She was always welcomed by the sick, who took comfort from her visits.

Lorena was not one to pity herself or to remain longer than necessary as a convalescent. She felt a great need to start working for the church, and to that end pleaded with her mother to arrange for an exam to obtain a prosthesis. Once she got it, Lorena joined a group of young people at her parish engaged in catechetical work. She was delighted when, in 1979, she was given her own class of youngsters. A dedicated teacher, she was beloved by her students, and reveled in realizing her belief that, as she put it, "Happiness will always be in serving the happiness of others, in being of service to others."

At the classical high school Pilo Albertelli in Rome, her companions remember Lorena as a true witness of the faith. It was with some of these friends and some of the young religion teachers that, in August 1980, she made a pilgrimage to Lourdes and bathed in the miraculous waters. While praying at the Grotto of Massabielle, Lorena fell into such deep prayer that her friends had difficulty in rousing her when it was time to rejoin the group. She wrote home saying that she was inspired by the suffering of so many, who bore their pain in silent prayer.

Between 1980 and early 1981, Lorena had the opportunity to live with the catechists and some other young people in a parish building. This experience of living, working, and praying with her companions contributed to her spiritual maturity and her rapid rise in sanctity. She wrote at this time, "I have understood that the most important thing is to live of love, to live for love, to live with love."

However, in January 1981, Lorena's happy life as a catechist was to come to an abrupt end when she was faced with another serious physical condition. The cancer she thought had been cured had metastasized instead, and in the process a tumor had destroyed her left lung. Her family and friends were devastated at the news, but she consoled them with a smile, saying, "Don't cry, but rejoice with me because if the good Lord thinks me worthy, I will join Him in eternal glory. This will be the greatest joy of all."

The doctors expected Lorena to live only three months. Lorena was aware when this was conveyed to her parents, and she somehow knew this prediction was true. Some physicians attempted various remedies — some even claimed Lorena was recovering — but she expected death and went serenely to the heavenly kingdom on April 3, 1981, at sixteen years and four months of age.

A scant eighteen years later, on October 4, 1999, her Cause for Beatification was introduced with the assignment of a postulator. The diocesan process was opened on May 25, 2001, with Camillo Cardinal Vicario Ruini proclaiming at the ceremony that Lorena must be presented as an example of holiness for the young. ✝

Venerable Maggiorino Vigolungo

1904 – 1918
14 years old
ITALY

$\mathcal{W}$hen the (future) Bl. James Alberione, the founder of the religious orders known as the Paulines, decided to help the people of the twentieth century by publishing and dispersing religious materials, he began by organizing a group of boys into an apostolate resembling a vocational technical school. The "Little Print Shop," also known as *Scuola tipografica editrice*, was begun in September 1913 and staffed in large part by these schoolboys, who lived and studied together under the good priest's spiritual direction. Among these boys was the outstanding Maggiorino Vigolungo, the son of humble farm workers.

He was born on May 6, 1904, in Benevello, Italy, a good-looking boy of lively intelligence who worked at being the first in schoolwork, games, and work. He attended elementary school in his native country but, at the age of twelve, met Fr. Alberione and was quickly inspired to help in the publication of religious materials for the good of the church. To Fr. Alberione, Maggiorino confided his dream: to become an apostle of the Catholic press, a priest, and then a saint. The boy once wrote, "With the grace of the Lord and the help of the Blessed Mother, I want to become a saint, a great saint, and a saint very soon." With Fr. Alberione as his spiritual director, Maggiorino was well on his way to realizing his dream.

As a member of the Society of St. Paul, he learned the operation of the printing presses and worked for hours at printing uplifting books and periodicals for distribution. When not engaged with the other boys in prayer, work, or studies, he would go out onto the streets handing out leaflets containing a spiritual message. He was, in reality, a saintly newsboy for God.

Maggiorino was delighted with his vocation and grew each day in the love of God. Especially attracted to the Holy Eucharist, he was determined to advance in virtue and accepted as his motto, "Progress, a little every day." He was faithful to this resolution and made swift progress in virtue and apostolic dedication.

One of the teachers who witnessed Maggiorino's rapid advance in virtue was the Rev. Timothy Giaccardo, the first general vicar of the Society of St. Paul. (Fr. Giaccardo's Cause for Beatification has been introduced. He now holds the title of Servant of God.)

Soon after his fourteenth birthday, Maggiorino became seriously ill, and Father Alberione asked him if he wanted to get well or go to heaven. The boy answered simply, "I desire to do the will of God."

He returned to his family when he was diagnosed with pleurisy, but later, when he was found to be suffering from meningitis, his friends joined in three days of intense prayer. On the last day of prayer, July 27, 1918, Maggiorino answered the call of God and joined Him in heaven. His last words to his companions were, "Pray that we may find each other all together in Paradise."

He was first buried in the cemetery at Benevello; then, in October 1933, his remains were exhumed and reinterred in a grave in Alba belonging to the Society of St. Paul. When the remains had to be officially recognized (a procedure required for the introduction of his Cause), the remains were again exhumed in 1962 and were brought with all religious fervor to the Church of St. Paul in Alba, where they were placed in a vault.

Maggiorino's dream of becoming a saint will be realized in due time, since Pope John Paul II approved the *Decree Super Virtutibus* in 1988, elevating the young boy to the ranks of Venerable. ✝

Venerable Mari Carmen Gonzalez–Valerio

1930 – 1939
9 years old
SPAIN

*D*escriptions of this child, as told by those who knew her well, give us this picture of her:

> She had a clear and alert intelligence. She was profoundly sincere, of sound judgment, persevering fervor, exquisite sensibility... always conscious and responsible for her actions. She was a completely normal girl with a strong character. She was very intelligent. She was not an outgoing person, but always truthful with anyone who asked.

Her Aunt Sofie, with whom Mari Carmen was very close, tells us she was "upright in spirit, strong of will, clear of mind, profoundly sincere. She was forceful but always balanced in judgment... determined in her way of acting, alertly sensitive, clear in her judgments and very correct in her decisions."

And then there is this: "She was very much a child... very much a child," who played with dolls and begged for sweets.

Her Aunt Sofie added, however: "The only defect she had, if it was indeed a defect, was the way her strong character would react immediately, and then take control." Even her mother agreed that Mari Carmen was different from her siblings.

She was born in Madrid on April 16, 1930, the second child of Don Julio Gonzalez-Valerio, an engineer on a railroad, and Doña Carmen Saenz de Heredia. Just as the Little Flower's home was one of deep spirituality, so was that of Mari Carmen. Her parents maintained a deep devotion to the Mother of God and fasted every Saturday in her honor. Her mother consecrated Mari Carmen, while still in the womb, to the Blessed Virgin during a novena to Our Lady of Mount Carmel. As a special sign of this consecration, she promised she would dress the child always in blue and white until the age of three. Mari Carmen's birth, however, was difficult; as an infant, she became gravely ill and was baptized immediately in her own home.

On the special initiative of the Papal Nuncio in Spain, Msgr. Federico Tedeschini, Mari Carmen received the sacrament of Confirmation when she was only two years old; she received her first Holy Communion when she was only six years old, on the feast of Our Lady of Perpetual Help, a special devotion of her father. In preparation for this event she would enter the chapel, greet Our Lord, and tell Him what she was doing.

Her mother noticed that after receiving her first Holy Communion, "She began to show signs of real sanctity." From then on, she began to attend Mass and receive Communion practically ever day. Later, when she was at school in Zalla, she would get up very early to assist at the nuns' Holy Mass and, after her Communion, she would make a fervent thanksgiving.

Only twenty days after Mari Carmen's Holy Communion, the Spanish Civil War began, bringing with it religious persecution, especially against Catholics. On the feast of the Assumption, August 15, 1936, Communist militants took her father before a terrorist tribunal. Julio, it seems, had once served in the army as an artilleryman, but had left the army in 1929 while the country was still under the monarchy.

As he was leaving the house, he called out, "When the children are older tell them that their father fought and gave his life for God and for Spain, so that they can be educated in a Catholic Spain with the Crucified One presiding in the schools." Julio did return later that night, only to be taken again a few days later. After this second arrest, the mother was in the cellar when she heard her husband shout, "Carmen, Carmen," from a truck passing by. A short time later her husband was assassinated for being a Catholic.

Because her mother was now in danger of arrest, she sought asylum in the Belgian Embassy and entrusted her children to the care of their Aunt Sofia. When her aunt worried about the situation, Mari Carmen would say to her, "Don't be upset. Let's say the rosary and recall Jesus' wounds." When the five children were threatened with being taken to Russia (to be educated in Marxism) on the feast of Our Lady of Lourdes, February 11, 1937, they instead joined their mother in the embassy. The military truck arrived at their house only minutes after they left.

Eventually, the family left the embassy and set sail for San Sebastian, where Mari Carmen first attended a school run by the Religious of the Sacred Heart, then became a boarding student in a school run by Irish nuns in Zalla. She was then six years old.

The child expressed her love of holy purity by always being modestly dressed, to the point where she would not even undress in the presence of her grandmother. She was also very charitable. If beggars came to the door asking for alms, she would contribute out of her own savings, then invite them to return when her mother could give them more. She was also fond of contributing her own clothing. Her grandmother remembers giving Mari Carmen money to buy toys or other things, but the little girl would give the money to the landlady to buy toys for her children instead, telling her not to say anything to her family.

Her mother remembers that Mari Carmen was extremely caring — "She always obeyed at once" — and honest; her grandmother reports, "I never remember her telling a lie." Anxious to spread the word of God, she gave spiritual classes to her dolls, teaching them to pray and make the Sign of the Cross with special fervor.

She loved to lead the family rosary and knew from memory the Litany of the Blessed Virgin in Latin. She was also devoted to the Rosary of the Lord's Wounds and especially loved the devotion to the Sacred Heart. She even bought promotional literature from her own savings to distribute to passersby.

Once when she was in deep conversation with a friend of the family who had been a Carmelite in Lisieux, her grandmother asked why they were talking so much. Mari Carmen answered seriously, "Grandmother, we are discussing mystical subjects." She was also very interested in the missions and offered little mortifications for them. While in school in Zalla, she made the Spiritual Exercises with her fellow students. At the end, the priest who had conducted the retreat asked one of the nuns about Mari Carmen. He then added, "That child is filled with the Holy Spirit."

Mari Carmen was indeed a very spiritual child. This is noted in her "diary," which she kept in an envelope sealed with adhesive tape. On the envelope she wrote three times, "Private." Her little secret was revealed when the envelope was opened after her death. Among other little notations were *Viva España* and *Viva Cristo Rey*, words on the lips of many martyrs during the war. What seems most important of all, though, was this notation: "I surrendered myself in the parish church of the Buen Pastor, April 6, 1939." The good Lord accepted this surrender: the infection that claimed her life began fifteen days later.

Mari Carmen forgave her father's assassins, and was profoundly interested in their eternal salvation, especially that of the president of the Republic, Azaña. This man, she reasoned, was the symbol of the whole religious persecution. Her mother relates that Mari Carmen prayed the Rosary of the Divine Wounds every day for the conversion of her father's murderers. She once said to her aunt, "Let us pray for Papa and for those who killed him." (Her prayers were apparently answered: Azaña had a profound religious conversion and died during the child's illness.)

While at school in Zalla, Mari Carmen contracted scarlet fever, soon accompanied by an infection of the ear and the mastoid. Unfortunately, the infection degenerated into septicemia that settled in the heart and kidneys.

Some time earlier, her grandmother had asked her if she wanted to be a saint, and did she know what that meant? Mari Carmen replied, "To be a saint, you have to mortify yourself." Mari Carmen did, indeed, mortify herself, through her sufferings.

She indicated at the beginning of her illness that she knew she would suffer and that she would die as a result of her condition. When prompted by her mother to ask the Child Jesus for a cure, Mari Carmen answered, "No, mama, I don't ask for that, I ask that His will be done."

Taken to Madrid on May 27, she was subject to an emergency mastoid operation and a thrombectomy. When she did not improve after a week, the doctors knew her condition was hopeless, yet they tried every available procedure.

One of her nurses tells us, "When they brought her from the clinic she was suffering a great deal with septicemia. . . . She had open sores. We had to give her blood serum twice a day and many injections. Some days there were more than 20. One of the things she suffered from especially [was] colitis, which she had continuously and very severely."

Every half hour, her caregivers gave Mari Carmen food which they hoped would cure the colitis; it was unappetizing, and she had difficulty in swallowing it, but she took it obediently without complaint. When asked what she would like to eat, she replied, "Whatever you think best." Often, before a painful treatment, she would ask everyone present to pray the Creed and the Our Father. Then she submitted without a word.

Another complication to her already serious condition was phlebitis, producing gangrenous wounds on her thighs. Just moving the bed sheets caused her torment. She was also feverish and suffered from insomnia. Sometimes, she could not suppress a cry of pain, especially during an injection or a transfusion. Afterward she would always say, "You, doctor, and everybody, please excuse me."

Doctor Antonio Martin Caldenin tells of her heroic patience: "During all that time and despite her nine years, this little girl endured all that pain and suffering with a truly exemplary resignation. It was extraordinary to observe how, when we would try some remedy or apply an injection, very painful procedures, especially in her state, all we had to do was to say 'Jesus' in order for her to endure it without complaint and without moving, something we doctors had never encountered in one so young."

Now and then someone would bring her a storybook, thinking to take her mind off her sufferings, but the only book she opened was a devotional book for children. She often opened it to a picture of an angel bringing a child to heaven. She never missed her customary prayers except once, when she was almost in a coma; upon her recovery from that state, she was very remorseful for having missed her prayers.

While enduring all this pain, she often asked her mother to sing a hymn sung during her first Holy Communion Mass, "How good you are, Jesus. How good you are." One line reads, "I want to love you with all my heart. How good you are, how good you are!"

Mari Carmen often predicted that the Blessed Mother would come for her on her feast day, July 16, that of Our Lady of Mount Carmel. But when she learned that her beloved Aunt Sofia was to be married on that day, she said she would die the next day. Before her wedding, Aunt Sofia visited her and said that after the ceremony she would bring her wedding flowers to the hospital. Mari Carmen replied, "No, Aunt Sofia. Just send me the lilies. I am going to need them."

A few days before she died, she confessed two little faults and asked for holy Viaticum and the Sacrament of the Sick.

When July 17 dawned, Mari Carmen sat up in her bed, something she had previously been unable to do, and announced joyfully, "Today I am going to die! Today I am going to heaven!" All that day she spoke of dying and of meeting her father in heaven; she even asked if her mother had a message for him. Some moments before dying, she looked at her relatives gathered around her bed and advised them, "Love one another." She then wondered if others heard the beautiful singing and asked who they might be. Her grandmother told her, "They are angels, Mari Carmen."

The child answered, "Yes, indeed. They are the angels who have come for me." She then said with a smile, "I am going to heaven. I am going without passing through Purgatory because I have been a martyr at the hands of the doctors. I die a martyr." Then joining her hands she said, "Jesus, Mary, and Joseph, assist me in my last agony. Jesus, Mary, and Joseph, grant that when I die, I die in peace and my soul comes to be with you." She died at three o'clock in the afternoon. She was nine years old.

Mari Carmen's face and head had been badly disfigured by the illness, but immediately after dying, her appearance changed so dramatically that one of her uncles exclaimed, "See how beautiful she looks." Everyone was enraptured by the change and by a sweet aroma that came, not from the flowers in the room, but from her body. In fact, she appeared so beautiful, with her body perfectly flexible, that the forensic doctor hesitated to certify her death, saying, "The child has to be dead, but this is no corpse."

They dressed Mari Carmen in her white first Communion dress and placed lilies from her aunt's wedding around the body. That evening, one of the doctors urged them to remove the flowers and place them in water so that they would be fresh for the burial, so the family removed some and left others around her face. The following morning, the flowers in water were wilted, but those around her face were as fresh as though they had just been gathered from a garden; they were covered with a mysterious mist said to have preserved them.

Before the funeral two days later, one of the doctors noted, "She showed no signs of rigidity, and she showed marvelous color and general appearance. Her face was rosy among the fresh lilies." Mari Carmen was buried in the church of the monastery of the Discalced Carmelites, in Aravaca, Madrid.

The reports of her sanctity began soon after burial, although the diocesan process for her beatification was opened 22 years later, on July 11, 1961. Biographies of the little girl soon followed, as well as an impressive list of favors received through her intercession. Her Cause was sent to Rome in 1983. The decree of approval was signed in 1985, and she was declared Venerable in 1996. +

Venerable Maria Carmelina Leone

1923 – 1940
17 years old
SICILY

The children of the Leone family lived in Palermo under modest circumstances. Despite their many hardships, their parents were exemplary Catholics, known throughout the neighborhood for their intense piety. Maria benefited from their example and, since early childhood, displayed a constant and faithful love of prayer.

Realizing that she was called to a higher level of virtue, her parents entrusted her to the protection of Our Lady of Mount Carmel. Since then, to the end of her life, she was faithful in wearing the scapular, which she considered a beloved garment of the Virgin Mary. Under the direction of the Jesuit Gaspare Giacalone, she advanced quickly in the way of perfection and became active in teaching the faith among the people of her district. She served as catechist in the church of the Jesuits and in nearby parishes, and became a member of the Apostolate of Prayer.

Maria was adept at embroidery and, after studying at a trade school, worked as a tailor. In her workplace and among her companions, she was considered an elegant soul of delicate religious sensibilities. She would have liked to serve God in the religious life, but this dream was put aside when she was found to be suffering from tuberculosis. She was sheltered for a time in a sanatorium but did not respond to medications, and was later returned home to die.

Said to have lived in a continuous dialogue with God and the Blessed Virgin, she was contemplative according to the Carmelite spirit. Toward the end of her life, she began to predict future events, including the day of her own death — and once advised those who knew her, "When I am up there in heaven, call me in all your needs. I will be present and I will pray for all of you." After suffering heroically under the most pious circumstances, she succumbed to the disease on October 10, 1940. Shortly after her death, she began to be known as the "holy, afflicted one."

She was first buried in the cemetery of the Rotoli, and later in that of the Capuchins. But soon, a spontaneous popular cult developed around her, with countless people visiting both at her grave and her parents' home. Many of these visitors suffered physically and morally but were spiritually enriched by their visits, and edified by the life of this simple but pious seventeen-year-old girl. Eventually Maria Carmelina became known throughout Sicily and beyond, with the devotion of her clients being rewarded with favors of all sorts.

Because of the increasing popular devotion for Maria Carmelina, the Archbishop of Palermo, Cardinal Salvatore Papalardo, and church authorities took notice and opened the inquiry for the process of beatification. The Decree of Heroic Virtues was declared on April 8, 1997, giving Maria Carmelina the title of Venerable. The "holy, afflicted one" now awaits beatification. ✝

Servant of God Maria (Puma)
a Columna Cimadevilla y Lopez–Doriga

1952 – 1962
10 years old
SPAIN

This saintly ten-year-old was born on February 17, 1952, to a devout Catholic family, the father being Amaro Cimadevilla and the mother, Maria del Rosario Lopez-Doriga, residents of Madrid. Of their seven children, only four survived childhood.

From her earliest years Puma, as she was affectionately called, was reflective, nostalgic, and sensitive by nature, but always had a deep love of church and neighbor. Her little acts of mortification were remarkable with her life being one of intense love and gratitude, even as early as four years of age, when she began to suffer various physical ailments. Nevertheless, Puma was able to attend school at the usual age and applied herself to her studies, excelling especially in her Catechism lessons and those concerning the history of the church. Puma was very fond of the sisters at the School of the Religious of Christ the King and delighted to be in their company.

Puma was described as being a very elegant child, naturally beautiful in spirit, who spoke slowly and very sweetly. A normal little girl, she liked to dress well, took good care of her belongings, and had a keen intelligence. She loved to play games with her siblings and schoolmates and exercised charity in an extraordinary way by often ending a game before her opponents lost — to spare them disappointment at not having won.

The sisters at the school remember that, when Puma was very little, she told them she wanted to make the Religious Exercises with her sister, Magdalene, two years older and in a different class. But the nuns were unable to grant her childish desire by making an exception in her case, since other children would also want to avail themselves of this exception. Deeply disappointed, Puma had trouble resigning herself to being denied permission; the sisters later found her sitting in a dark corner.

Her love of the Child Jesus was intense and sincere. When asked what she wanted to be when she grew up, she invariably replied that she wanted to be the spouse of the Child Jesus. One of the nuns who taught her remembers that Puma once said she wanted to be the little companion of the Child Jesus.

When it came time to prepare herself for her first Holy Communion, she studied with a deep seriousness that edified both the sisters and her parents. While her Communion dress, the veil, and her flowered crown were being prepared, Puma displayed a remarkable lack of vanity; she was said to have told her mother, in all seriousness, that clothes were of no importance, only her union with Jesus mattered.

The ceremony took place on May 15, 1959, in a small chapel of the Church of San Ginés. From that day onward Puma's interest was in pleasing God by receiving the Holy Eucharist as often as possible. Frequently, mother and daughter were seen walking together to the Church of San Ginés to receive the holy Body of Christ.

Around this time, however, Puma's physical condition began to deteriorate. After days of medical examinations and tests, the parents, suspecting a mere childhood illness, were distraught when the doctors determined that the seven-year-old was suffering from the malignant disorder of Hodgkin's disease, with its accompanying fatigue, loss of weight, fever, and pain.

The parents need not have worried about Puma's reaction to the doctors' omnious verdict, however. She was known to have whispered to her mother, "I offer my life to Jesus." Those who witnessed the child's reaction declared among themselves that the Holy Spirit was inspiring her. Her pleasant acceptance of her suffering and her serenity in facing her forthcoming death inspired the hospital chaplain, the nuns from the school, and the medical personnel. Those who knew of her willing acceptance of God's will frequently visited the sick child to receive encouragement in their own trials. Everyone who came in contact with Puma marveled at her extraordinary capacity to deal with her condition in a spiritual manner. While Puma was able to attend school, even her classmates were edified.

From the day of her entrance into the hospital, Puma became the object of attention and the darling of the hospital personnel. All were amazed at her pleasant disposition and the smiling resignation of her condition. The sisters who cared for her declared, "Everything in Puma was extraordinary. . . . She possessed a fine humility and an exquisite charity . . . and other qualities that distinguish the saints."

During Puma's hospitalization, her parents began to prepare her soul for heaven by speaking of God's love of children, the end of all created things, the infinite kindness of God, and the eternal bliss of heaven. These worthy parents succeeded in preparing their child for sainthood — this evidenced by Puma's saying to her father, "Papa, I want you to promise me an important thing, and that you will always do it, even if I don't die. It is that you continue to go frequently to Holy Mass and to take Communion, even if you have to get up very early."

Puma need not have worried. Her parents were very religious and recited the rosary every evening in their home. Puma loved this religious exercise and would spring toward her mother when the time came for prayer. The child also had a great fondness for the lives of the saints, contemplating their graces and sufferings. She once mentioned to her mother that, like the saints, she must suffer for her little transgressions, but that it was good that Jesus gave her sufferings since God the Father sent sufferings to His own son. "All should be joyfully accepted."

Puma's love and respect of the Holy Eucharist displayed maturity beyond her years. Every evening, in preparation for receiving the Eucharist the next morning, Puma began her prayers the night before with great devoutness. One can only imagine her happiness and thankfulness the next morning when she was united with the love of her pure heart. On days when she could not receive Holy Communion, she nevertheless prayed the rosary with her mother, even though her little body was exhausted from fever and pain.

She fully knew the incurable nature of her illness. One evening, as she prepared to pray the rosary in the company of her mother and an aunt, she turned to an image of the Child Jesus and said aloud, "Jesus, this rosary I offer for this intention: since there is no cure, may it do well for my soul, and may your sacred will be done."

At night, when her sufferings were less severe, the night watchman, the nurses, and sometimes her doctor would find her kneeling at the foot of her bed in deep prayer, oblivious of all around her. The doctor remarked that her beautiful expression at such times gave ample testimony of the depth of her spiritual life.

One of her nurses reported that Puma never despaired for a moment; it amazed them that a child of nine years was so calm, sweet, and smiling in the face of illness. "It reveals a power outside the common," the nurse said, "and it confers a high spiritual value to the strength that showed in her acceptance of suffering."

As if her sufferings were not enough, Puma continued to practice voluntary sacrifices, such as delaying refreshment offered during a feverish night and accepting it only in the morning. When her parents installed a television set as a means of distracting their child from her suffering, this was an avenue for other sacrifices. If they were watching a program that she did not like, or one that annoyed her, Puma never showed her displeasure. Instead she would close her eyes or cover her head with the sheet.

Throughout her illness Puma remained thankful for all services rendered, becoming visibly annoyed only if she heard words of criticism regarding someone. Witnesses affirm that she was extremely kind to her visitors and forgot her own pain when someone with an affliction visited her. She always inquired about their health and promised to pray for them.

One of her doctors later testified, "I have followed with great care the physical condition of this nine-year-old child. Everyone loved to enter her room because of her angelic smile. She never spoke of her illness, neither of the pain, neither of death; but rather, her happy longing for heaven, all of which indicated the greatness of her soul. Were it not for the results of laboratory tests, one would not believe she endured fever or pain. She impressed me profoundly."

One of the nuns who frequently visited her remarked how interested Puma was in the missions. She once told this nun in all confidence that she prayed her fatigue, offered up, would somehow relieve a missionary experiencing exhaustion. Her heartfelt interest was also extended to saving sinners, and it was for this intention that she once said she had offered her life.

When Puma heard of an organization known as the Union of Infirm Missionaries — sick who offered their sufferings for foreign missionaries — she joined immediately, content that her sufferings were united with those of Jesus on the cross. She prayed for the capacity to accept future sufferings, invoking the Heavenly Father to increase vocations to missionary fields.

Days before she died, she heard of a poor invalid man in need of a wheelchair. Puma instructed her mother to give her small savings to two Sisters of the Poor who had treated her, so that this elderly man would have what he needed. After Puma's death, her mother performed this kindness for her.

Puma died on March 6, 1962, and was buried in the cemetery of Carabanchel. Her classmates sang during the funeral Mass, while the sisters of the hospital carried the casket to its crypt.

All those who knew Puma — neighbors, teachers, classmates, and hospital personnel — gave ample testimony of the child's holiness; only one year after her death, the Process of Beatification of this *Enferma Missionari* was solemnly initiated by the bishop of Madrid and a large number of distinguished members of the clergy. In accordance with the requirements of the process, Puma's remains were exhumed and identified in March 1966. They were then transferred to a crypt in the parish church of St. Ginés, the site of her first Holy Communion, and where she had so often received the Holy Eucharist.

The application for the beatification of ten-year-old Maria a Columna Cimadevilla y Lopez-Doriga was deemed worthy, and was accepted by the Congregation for the Causes of Saints in 1986. ✝

Maria Cristina Ogier

1955 – 1974
19 years old
ITALY

She was devoted to the well-being of others, the missions, the sick, the unborn, and especially expectant mothers experiencing difficulties in their lives. What this young girl accomplished, in nineteen short years, to help the sick in the mission field is truly astounding; what she left undone goes on through the efforts of the many people inspired by her ideals and love of charity. Thus, her dreams for the welfare of the sick, the elderly, and the unborn are still being realized.

Maria Cristina, born in Florence on March 9, 1955, was the only child of Dr. Henry Ogier, an obstetrician and gynecologist, and Gina Matteoni, both devout Catholics. She was a beautiful and healthy child until the age of four, when she contracted a common childhood illness but, contrary to expectaions, did not recover completely. Instead, she began to drag her right foot when walking. Many doctors examined the child and concluded that she had a tumor on the brain.

Not knowing whether or not Maria Cristina would survive an operation, her parents thought it best to prepare her for her first Holy Communion. The parish priest, Don Setti — her spiritual director for life — undertook that preparation. She studied enthusiastically and received the sacrament on April 30, 1961.

Five months later, Maria Cristina went to Lourdes for the first time. She went in a wheelchair and drank the water from the little cups commonly used by the sick. Don Setti, her parents, and a group of pilgrims accompanied her. One of her doctors had predicted that there might be a period of seeming improvement — and so it was, since she appeared to be free of pain and apparently cured.

Soon, she was attending the elementary classes taught by the Sisters in Santa Reparata, who noticed how eagerly she hurried each morning to their chapel to make a visit to the Blessed Sacrament before beginning her classes. It was at this time that her teacher, Mara Cappelli, noted the child's virtues and aspirations for the future; even at this tender age, Maria hoped to become a doctor to help the sick. Her teacher wrote:

> I first met Maria Cristina when at the age of six she began her school life, and already her heart vibrated with love of God and her neighbour [sic].
>
> Incapable of envy, jealousy, [or] rancor, even at school she was always ready to rejoice and suffer with the others, to lend a helping hand, to understand and make excuses for the others, she, who more than all the others needed to be helped, understood, and excused.
>
> She studied with diligence and honesty, never expecting any concessions, aware of her duty to apply herself with all her capacity; she studied in order to enrich herself, but above all in view of the good she hoped one day to do for the sick who were most abandoned and most in need, once she had attained her degree in medicine.

In her effort to make herself more acceptable to God, she tried to correct her shortcomings and little human failings: the negative aspects of her character for which life with its trials was partly responsible.

Deep down, Maria Cristina was a child like any other. Like her companions she loved life, friendships, sport and all the good things that life had to offer. But nevertheless, she always kept aflame in herself the light of grace and worked tenaciously for the Lord in a way quite exceptional for one so young.

At the age of seven, Maria Cristina once again began to limp slightly. She was taken from one shrine to another and even went with Don Setti to visit Padre Pio on several occasions (including the last day of St. Pio's life on earth). Her pain continued, however.

In spite of this, her mother noticed that Maria Cristina apparently did not pray for herself. The child once remarked, "There are many suffering more than I am, and they are also poor, and I am short of nothing." Again, when asked if she prayed to the Madonna for a cure, Maria Cristina replied, "No, Mamma, I prayed for the salvation of the world."

Maria Cristina never underwent the delicate operation that might cure the condition; doctors doubted it would be successful, and it might have even been fatal. She bravely continued her studies, tolerating the difficulties involved. In spite of this, when she reached the age of about thirteen, she helped organize Prayer Groups first in St. John's Church and later in St. Lawrence's Basilica. Her prayer life and advance in virtue were deeply influenced by the sermons given by her spiritual director, who encouraged her to receive the Eucharist on a daily basis.

It was under Don Setti's guidance that groups of teenagers began working in various fields of charity: the missions, hospitals, prisons, and the House of Hope for needy families. Meetings were often held for the spiritual formation of the members, and every month the entire group of workers attended a day's retreat. Here, Maria Cristina found her calling, at about fourteen or fifteen years of age. She was to take part in the hospital group.

There was only one difficulty — she was attracted to a handsome young man, a member of her group. She expressed her affection for him in her private writings and, with maturity beyond her years, ended her remarks with these words: "I loved you because you taught me to love Him, but now I love Him and Him alone." Because of this young man's presence in her group, she left and instead joined the Mission Group.

Around this time she had a teacher, Giustina Grisola Mannelli, who recorded this remembrance of Maria Cristina:

> She was one of many girls to whom I taught Latin and Greek, but with her the relationship was different because she was different from the other girls. I was always impressed by her great spirit, her tenacity, and her desire to be useful to others and to turn even her misfortunes to good account, to the best of her ability. . . . she was enthusiastic and had a zeal for charity . . . Maria Cristina had many problems and this was a misfortune which made her differ- ent from her companions and which deprived her of many joys common to girls of her age, and yet in her short life she succeeded in making the most of her talents, and of never wasting time. . . . She probably showed me the greatest proof of her self-abnegation at Lourdes where she took me and where she never stopped going even for a moment. On the train when all of us were tired and sleeping, she was one of the few who found the energy to work, going up and down the corridors to bring comfort to those who were worse off than herself. . . . She was transformed at Lourdes and found a source of exceptional energy because at Lourdes she could really be useful to someone and feel indispensable.

Unexpectedly, Maria Cristina was given an opportunity to help both the hospital and mission groups. A young doctor-priest, Fr. Pius Conti of the Capuchin Order, came to Florence for a refresher course in obstetrics under the direction of her father, Dr. Ogier. Maria Cristina was enthralled when the young priest told of the mission field in the Amazon, how there were neither roads, railways, nor airfields in the deep forest regions along the river. The only means of communication and transportation was the great river itself, where the *Indios* rowed their canoes. The sick and wounded were transported several miles by this primitive means to the little hospital of the Missioners. Many of them, the priest related, died on the way. "What is needed," he said, "is a boat with all the facilities for casualties and first aid. We need to raise funds to buy a boat that will travel the Amazon."

Maria Cristina's charity was immediately aroused. She was already exceptionally generous in the Young Community and, as an ex-patient, contributed what she could to the Orthopaedic Traumatological Centre. (It was said that she never saw a person in need without helping him or her by her charity.) This idea of acquiring a hospital boat set her immediately into action.

Even as she battled her headaches and coped with her studies, she wrote to everyone she knew: various religious organizations, newspapers, religious periodicals, churches, businesses, and schools. All in all it was a monumental undertaking, but her persistence paid off when donations came in to purchase the boat. Many of her adult friends helped out to obtain various medical testing equipment and supplies so that, in the end, this boat had all capability for emergency and medical use plus beds for the convalescents. It was, in reality, a veritable floating clinic.

On the day it was given to the Capuchin Order for its use on the Amazon, a picture was taken of the Ogier family in front of the boat, aptly named the *Maria Cristina*. It continues to sail the Amazon to this day.

At this time, Maria Cristina was still receiving Holy Communion every day and praying at length. Each night after the family rosary, her mother would find her on her knees. But to suggestions that she should go to bed, Maris Cristina once replied, "I must still pray for the whole world, for the missions, for Don Setti . . . for Fr. Pius . . . for the sick . . ."

Her great love for Our Lord's Passion enabled her to keenly feel the problems of the world, and she prayed for them all: for peace, for families, and for her greatest longing of all, the conversion of sinners. She also had a great love of Our Lady and was attracted to St. Francis. After reading his life, she expressed the desire to become a Franciscan tertiary, and was admitted into the Third Order during a Mass celebrated in the Capitular Chapel on October 10, 1973. It was in this chapel only a few months previously that she had — in spite of her weakness — cleaned the floor and the benches.

Maria Cristina still dreamed of being a member of the medical profession and made plans for her future. "I'll be a doctor; I'll be a pediatrician; I'll dedicate myself to children; I'll go to the mission field," she would say, even while at the same time expressing the opinion that she would not live past the age of eighteen or nineteen.

Finally, she became so weak she was obliged to lean on her mother's arm while walking and could no longer stand steadily. Refusing to give in to her affliction, she enrolled in the Faculty of Medicine at the university and even attended several lectures. But even as she began this education, she was becoming unusually tired, absent-minded, and inattentive. The tumor in the center of Maria Cristina's brain was almost the same size as it had been, but her leg still dragged, and she continually supported her right hand with her left.

In hopes of trying to secure a special cure, her mother brought her to Rome. One day, Maria Cristina attended Holy Mass and received Communion, as was her custom. She was sitting down at the breakfast table, stretching out her arm to her mother, when suddenly the arm went limp, and she suffered a bulbar paralysis that ended her life.

Her body was brought back from Rome on January 10 and placed in the chapel of the Stigmata of St. Francis in St. Lawrence's Square. The funeral was held the next afternoon. Among the concelebrants were four Franciscans from Assisi. In the presence of her family and friends, Maria Cristina was laid to rest on the hill of San Miniato, in the cemetery of Porte Sante.

During her brief life, she often visited the sick and patiently listened to their litanies of problems. After visiting a nursing home, she became depressed at the conditions endured by the residents and conceived the idea of establishing houses with better maintenance and more sensitive, caring workers. This dream was fulfilled after her death, when those inspired by her ideals established a foundation. The foundation raised funds for a nursing home, established as the Maria Cristina Home in Viale Galilei. Funds are also being collected for a day hospital and for the refueling of the boat *Maria Cristina*. A home for young girls has also been established, in Maria Cristina's memory, operated by sisters of the Minims of the Sacred Heart order.

The dream she had of establishing homes for pregnant women experiencing serious economic and social difficulties was fulfilled by her father as the Center of Aid to Life, offering alternatives to abortion. In 1986, Pope John Paul II visited the Center and spoke with the father at length about his saintly daughter. ✝

St. Maria Goretti

1890 — 1902
12 years old
ITALY

From the very beginning, the Goretti family suffered the bitter pangs of poverty. Maria's mother, Assunta, was an orphan who had never learned to read or write. Maria's father, Luigi, after finishing his tour of military service, returned to Corinaldo, Italy, married Assunta, and began to farm for a living. Our saint, the third child of this marriage, was born on October 16, 1890. She was baptized the day after her birth and received the names of Maria Teresa.

The small piece of land farmed by Luigi proved incapable of supporting his family despite his hard work. Eventually, when Maria was six years old, the family's situation became so critical that Assunta and Luigi made plans to move from Corinaldo and settled at Colle Gianturco, near Rome, where they stayed for two years farming a piece of land with the help of the Cimarelli family. In later years Assunta revealed that their condition there was no better than it had been before — they were forced most of the time to "live off chestnut flour pudding and maize bread."

When the family became acquainted with the Serenelli family, which consisted of the father, Giovanni, and his son, Alessandro, all three families journeyed to Ferriere di Conca, a place near Nettuno. Here the Serenelli and Goretti families shared a farmhouse called La Cascina Antica, while the Cimarelli family lodged in a newer house nearby. All three families agreed to work the land of Count Mazzoleni. Unfortunately, malaria was rampant in that area of the countryside and, as a result, many died. Luigi contracted the disease one year and three months after he and his family arrived there and succumbed to it when he was only 41. His widow, 35, was left with six children. The eldest child was twelve years old; the youngest was three months.

Assunta was forced to take her husband's place in the fields while Maria, then nine and a half years old, willingly and generously assumed the duties of the household and the care of the children. She also assumed the household chores of the Serenelli family. Her daily work consisted of fetching water each day from the fountain, washing and mending clothes, and going to the Village of Conca to buy household provisions. From time to time she went to Nettuno — a hot journey in the summer, and a muddy one in winter — to sell eggs and chickens. With the money she received for them, she would buy what the family needed, according to her mother's orders. At least she had company for the trips; usually, she walked to Nettuno with members of the Cimarelli family. While in Nettuno, they would visit the shrine of Our Lady of Graces to confess, attend Holy Mass, and receive Holy Communion.

Maria was always obedient and of a meek and loving disposition. She also possessed a spirit of mortification, suffering in silence the shortage — and sometimes the absence — of food. When she received sweets from neighbors, she always brought them home to share with the other children. On one occasion, when Maria was doing her customary marketing, a merchant gave her an apple and a sugar cookie, which she slipped into her bag. When the merchant asked why she was saving them, Maria replied that they were for her brothers and sisters.

Maria remained uneducated, her diet was meager, and her responsibilities went far beyond what was considered bearable for one of her age. Yet Assunta could not relieve her little family of their squalid situation, since Giovanni Serenelli kept most of the profits from their hard work.

Nevertheless, Maria was a cheerful child by habit, uncomplaining regardless of what was asked of her. In addition to her inherent goodness, Maria was also a beautiful child with light chestnut hair. Her intelligence was also obvious to everyone, as was a certain refinement and a delicacy of personality out of place in the drabness of the Marshes.

Though Maria was poor in earthly possessions, she was wealthy in the love of the Catholic faith. From all indications, her sanctity is attributable to the care her mother took in teaching her the basics of the faith and the way of virtue. In addition to lessons from her mother, Maria derived great benefit from the sermons of the parish priest at Sunday Mass and from the training she received prior to her first Holy Communion, which she received on June 29, 1901. For this occasion, caring neighbors provided her clothing and accessories. According to custom, Maria had already received the sacrament of Confirmation at an earlier time.

The prayer life of the little family was once described by Assunta: "At home we would close the day by reciting the Holy Rosary, except during summer when sometimes we couldn't manage it, as there was so much work to do. Little Maria never missed it; and after her father's death, when we had already gone to bed, she would recite another five mysteries for the repose of his soul. She did this in addition because she knew that I couldn't have Masses celebrated, because I didn't have enough money."

Assunta's little family stayed faithful to the practice of virtue, but the Serenelli family was very different. In their part of the house, the father sought relief from his poverty through alcohol, while both the father and son amused themselves with pornographic magazines.

After a time, the twenty-year-old Alessandro Serenelli started to give Maria difficult chores to perform, then complain that they were not completed according to his orders. Sometimes Maria was reduced to tears, but she continued to do what was assigned to her. Unknown to Assunta, Alessandro then began to make improper advances to the future saint. Not wanting to burden her mother with another problem, Maria never spoke of it.

On the morning of July 5, 1902, Alessandro ordered Maria to mend one of his shirts. While her mother was busy threshing, Maria sat at the top of the stairs situated along the outside of the house and placed her little sister, Theresa, on a quilt beside her while she began to do the mending. After a time Alessandro, who had been working with Assunta, excused himself and left for the house. Climbing the stairs, he grabbed Maria, pulled her into the kitchen, produced a knife, and demanded that she submit to him. Protesting that it would be a sin against the law of God, and that if he did it he would go to hell, Maria refused to yield. In a rage, Alessandro stabbed her fourteen times in vital areas: the heart, lungs, and intestines.

The scuffle awakened little Theresa, who began to cry. When Assunta heard the baby, she sent her son Mariano to quiet Theresa and find Maria. Alessandro's father, standing in the shade at the bottom of the stairs, joined Mariano. Together they found Maria, mortally wounded, on the floor of the kitchen. Alessandro was in his room, pretending to be asleep.

Maria was rushed to the hospital in Nettuno, where the surgeons marveled that she was still alive and operated on the victim for two hours without administering an anesthetic. Because of her serious condition, she was not given the water she asked for, but she did receive Holy Communion, the Last Sacraments, and was received into an organization known as the Children of Mary. For 20 hours, Maria lay in excruciating pain, a model of perfect patience and forgiveness.

With her virginity preserved, she spent her last hours on earth praying and forgiving Alessandro for what he had done. "Do you forgive your murderer with all your heart?" she was asked. Maria replied, "Yes, for the love of Jesus I forgive him and I want him to be with me in Paradise."

Maria often turned her gaze toward an image of Our Lady during her final hours of life, and at the prompting of the chaplain she recited ejaculatory prayers. Just before the end came, she called, "Theresa," as though she had suddenly remembered the child she had left on the stair landing. After this, she calmly breathed her last. It was three o'clock, the sixth of July, 1902. Maria was eleven years, nine months, and twenty days old.

The little martyr of purity was buried in the cemetery at Nettuno, but later her remains were removed to the Shrine of Our Lady of Graces, where she had so often prayed and received the sacraments.

Alessandro was tried for the murder and received a prison sentence of 30 years.

For a time he remained unrepentant, but he at last experienced conversion during a vision of Maria who appeared to him in his prison cell. During this vision a garden appeared before him where a young girl with golden hair, clad in white, went about gathering lilies. He counted exactly fourteen of them, representing the number of wounds she had sustained; then she drew near him, with a smile, and encouraged him to accept the armful of flowers. As he did so, each lily was transformed into a still, white flame. Maria then disappeared.

After his release from prison, the now-repentant Alessandro first sought forgiveness from Maria's mother and then found employment as a gardener in a Capuchin monastery, where he worked until his death. He testified to Maria's sanctity during the Cause for Beatification, as did 30 other witnesses who had known her.

Maria was beatified on April 27, 1947, 45 years after her death. She was canonized on June 24 during the Holy Year of 1950. Because of the unprecedented crowd attending the ceremony, Pope Pius XII performed the canonization outdoors, the first such ceremony to be held outside St. Peter's Basilica. Present were Maria's brother and sister and her mother, Assunta, who had the distinction of witnessing the canonization of her child.

During the time of the beatification and canonization, a wax figure of the saint, which enclosed her bones, was taken to Rome in a glass-sided reliquary. There it was displayed to countless visitors in the Church of Sts. John and Paul. Later the relics were returned to Nettuno where they remain.

Included among the pilgrims who have visited these relics is Pope John Paul II, who traveled the 40 miles from Rome to Nettuno in September 1979. While in Nettuno, the Holy Father exhorted young people to look upon Maria Goretti as an example of purity to be emulated in this permissive society. The Holy Father also visited a 70-year-old Franciscan Missionary nun, Sr. Theresa, the sister of the saint.

Pilgrims often visit the Cascina Antica, the house where Maria Goretti lived for three years. It remains exactly as it was during the saint's lifetime. In the middle of the house on the upper floor is the kitchen where Maria was mortally wounded. A marble plaque indicates the exact place where she was found. Also seen here is a bronze bas-relief, the gift of Pope Pius XII, vividly recalling the saint's martyrdom. On the exterior of the house, the pilgrim can see the steps where Maria was mending Alessandro's shirt shortly before the martyrdom. One can also see the bedroom where she had slept in innocence, the threshing-floor where she had played with her brothers and sister, and the fountain where she had gone for water, as well as the exact location along the river where she washed clothes.

Maria Goretti, a poor, unschooled child, is the pride of modern Italy and a model of purity for the youth of the world. ✝

Servant of God Maria Lichtenegger

1906 – 1923
17 years old
AUSTRIA

*I*t is difficult to understand her father's reasoning, but at this saintly girl's birth on August 4, 1906, Maria Lichtenegger's father wished a "curse" on both mother and daughter to ensure that Maria would be the only daughter. Little did he realize that the daughter would someday be a candidate for the honors of the altar.

Born in St. Marein, Austria, Maria ended her elementary studies and was sent to a neighbor to learn sewing and needlework. In those days, before a seamstress worked professionally, she needed a certificate. (Ironically, the certificate was delivered to the family after Maria was already dead at the age of seventeen.)

Maria was an outstanding girl who had a perfect mastery of herself and was always serene and joyous. She was never seen to be idle; in her free moments she was busy with housework or needlework.

She manifested a deep and sincere devotion to the Mother of God and the veneration of the Blessed Eucharist, essential elements of her life.

She once acknowledged to her mother how much she loved God, saying, "I so infinitely love Jesus that every sacrifice for Him is easy, and to die for Him would be for me the greatest joy. When I am on my knees in adoration in front of the altar, the Savior talks to my soul." The mother revealed that once, while Maria was kneeling in front of the Blessed Sacrament, Our Lord spoke to her heart saying, "My daughter, when the most beautiful flowers, the roses and the lilies, bloom, you will come to my house and you will be with me."

This vision probably took place during the winter, as in May 1923, Maria was stricken with illness and the suffering that came with it. She demonstrated heroic patience, so much so that the physician told her parents, "If you knew how much she suffers! I have never seen such a case endured with so much patience. She is a true angel."

The priest who attended her during her final days revealed, "She sacrificed for those people who didn't love Jesus, that is, for the sinners and the infidels in pagan lands."

Maria died on July 8, 1923. Her Cause for Beatification was accepted in 1956. ✝

Servant of God Maria Orsola Bussone

1954 - 1970
15 years old
ITALY

*S*he played the guitar and was every bit a girl of her own time, with all the ambitions and interests of girls her age. But she was extraordinarily in love with Jesus, so that after her death, when Pope John Paul II was visiting Turin in September, 1988, he quoted her words to her confessor: "I'm prepared to give my life so that young people can understand how beautiful it is to love God." This was followed by sustained applause.

One biographer wrote that the life of Maria Orsola "is really an inspiring life, and we are only able to thank God to have given us this young girl as an example to the young people of Italy and the world — an example of a miraculous and inspiring life, lived in all of her fullness for God and for the church."

Maria was born in Vallo Torinese on October 2, 1954, and was a girl of high spirits and a ready smile. When she was almost thirteen years old, she eagerly joined the Focolare Movement, founded by Chiara Lubich, and dedicated herself to its religious and apostolate endeavors. Asked later about the Movement, why she joined it, and why she worked so hard in the parish, she answered, "To us young girls, we feel the need to have a family in which all love one another and where our problems are understood. I don't speak of the natural family. I speak of a spiritual family where our difficulties find answers, helping us to live the Word of life and to love Jesus with abandon."

This young girl with such deep feelings was also a good student, having earned a free tour of Luxemburg, Paris, and Rome as the winner of a scholastic contest.

She loved to play the guitar and sing little songs, but she reveals, "Great works, those of Beethoven, Chopin and Bach, I don't understand. What attracts me is the 'beat'... a flood of life." She did not like music played too loudly, and once asked some boys why they did so. The answers she received surprised her. One boy said, "I play this loud music to fill the void that I have in my soul." Maria Orsola was deeply saddened that God did not fill the emptiness they experienced.

One would never have suspected that the life of this energetic and joyful young girl would be cut short. But one day, while she was using a defective electrical appliance, she was electrocuted and died instantly.

She has always been remembered as a devout and prayerful young girl, but the depth of her spirituality was not really known until after her death, when a diary was found tucked among her schoolbooks. This diary, written during a period of three years, contains such inspiring thoughts that bishops and priests have noted its spiritual maturity and have written glowing remarks concerning it.

In this diary, after a time of trial, she wrote:

During Holy Mass I have lost every worry of mine to live the will of God in the present instant and I have told God that I was ready not to have any joy inside of me since He had little during His lifetime.

Another time she wrote:

I choose God and His cross. To this I have first of all thanked God for everything and I have told Him I am ready to join Him in suffering.

She once observed:

In us young people there is the wish to change the things that are not right... not with violence but with a life of giving. Many, in fact, are the young people that devote their leisure time to the neediest people, to the ones that suffer and if everybody sought the good in one another all the problems of social, moral and scientific order would be resolved... a world where all help each other and are loved, not caring of what color you are. Not even the place one occupies in society, but a new world where you don't feel only yourself and abandoned in the middle of the noise of cars, where you find happiness in a great family.

This journal shows in many ways that Maria Orsola seemed to have an intuition for, and an understanding of, life beyond her sixteen years.

Did Maria Orsola have a particular or favorite saint as a model? It appears not, as she writes, "In short I don't have a particular person that I try to imitate, but I try to know and then to assimilate what there is of the positive in all the people with whom I have the opportunity of a close friendship." In the Focolare Movement, Maria Orsola had many close friends who undoubtedly appreciated her virtues as much as she did theirs.

She also points out, "Everything should be for the glory of God... and in my mind I try to make well the things of every moment... in the small things of every day."

Maria died on July 10, 1970 at Treporti, Venice, Italy. Her grave is the destination of frequent visits not only by townspeople, but also by foreign bishops and tourists, since she is quickly becoming known throughout the world.

The Cause for Maria Orsola's Beatification was begun on May 26, 1996. The last action taken on it was in 1997. +

Servant of God Montserrat Grases

1941 – 1959
18 years old
SPAIN

Of the nine children born to Manuel and Manolita Grases, Montserrat — or Montse, as she was called — was the second born and was named in honor of Our Lady of Montserrat, a shrine of Our Lady that drew many pilgrims and devotees.

Although she ultimately didn't live long, Montse's life nearly was over before it began. When she was two years old, a wrong diagnosis of a bronchial condition and an incorrectly prescribed medication had her in serious condition for almost a month. That time, changing doctors and medications helped save her, but not without several crises in which she was not expected to live. Upon her recovery, the family moved from Barcelona to Seva, a little village near the city of Vich, where the child could benefit from the fresh air recommended by her doctor.

Once she was blooming with good health, Montse and the family returned to Barcelona, where she proved herself to be a cheerful child, jovial, very playful, and with a bit of a temper. In her early years,

Montse's mother reports, the child was like all little girls with her little likes and dislikes and that she "was not a holy child." The mother adds that she gave Montse the same formation as the other children.

"We taught them what we believe and struggle to put into practice.... We taught them right from the cradle to say some simple prayers, to develop a relationship with the Child Jesus, to have devotion to Our Lady, to accept and offer up pain, to struggle against one's own little defects, to help each other...." Manolita concludes, "We gave her a Christian upbringing, but what happened in Montse's soul was because God wanted it. It was the result of her correspondence to grace ... the fruit of God's grace and love."

When Montse was five years old, she began her studies at the Jesus and Mary School, first as a day student and then as a boarder. Years later, one of the nuns, Mother Anne, told Montse's mother that even at Montse's tender age, the child had made a deep impression on her. At the age of seven, Montse made her first Holy Communion.

Her father reports that Montse, as she was growing up, was a very lively little girl. "She was very balanced, joyful, and simple, and she was almost always calm" — her calm disturbed only by the little tantrums and scuffles normal between brothers and sisters in domestic situations. Her mother adds, "Montse was very straightforward.... She had no guile of any kind."

When she was ten years old, she attended the Dominican school named the Holy Child Jesus School. A contemporary of Montse remembers her playing ball during the morning break, as she was talented in all kinds of sports.

During those years, the country was recovering from the hardships of the war. Rationing was finally ending. Stalin died, and Elizabeth was crowned Queen of England. Undisturbed by the world changes, Montse continued to thrive, and her grades improved, although she "failed dismally" in literature. She attended the Music Academy and received honors in piano with distinction in music theory.

By the time Montse was out of sixth grade, there was one school activity that she particularly cherished: teaching Catechism to children in one of the working class suburbs of Barcelona. One teacher recalls, "I remember she used to go often on Sundays, so enthusiastically. She would take the children toys, books, and candy. . . ."

As one can imagine, rearing eight children wasn't easy economically, especially when the family's business almost failed. But somehow they managed, and eventually the children realized the sacrifices their parents were making to keep them in Catholic schools. Enrique, the eldest of the children, remembers that the financial difficulties taught the children "to work better at school, not to ask for unnecessary things, but rather to be happy with what we had. We were a happy family."

Manuel, Montse's father, was a very devout man who went to Mass often and made a retreat every year. When he expressed a desire to do more for the Church, he was introduced to people who belonged to Opus Dei. This organization, as we know, has developed into an apostolate in which thousands of men and women all over the world undertake their own progress in virtue and the care of others spiritually and materially.

At this time, members of Opus Dei would go to the Turo district, a very poor suburb of Barcelona, to help the poor who lived in shanty houses made from pieces of old wood. Opus Dei workers taught Catechism, set up a dispensary and a secondhand clothing shop, and helped in any way they could. Fr. Emilio Navarro introduced Manuel and Manolita to the work. In October 1954 Manolita visited Llar, a Center of Opus Dei. Here a few young ladies lived in community in very poor circumstances. Retreats were given here as well as meetings of university students, working people, and teenagers. A priest of Opus Dei would regularly visit to offer Holy Mass, hear confessions, preach, and give meditations. After services, there would be singing and laughter in a warm, family atmosphere.

The day that Manolita first visited Llar, she had picked up Montse from school and brought her daughter with her; thus Montse was introduced to the work of Opus Dei. There she met Rosa Pantaleoni, who had contracted polio and whose legs were so damaged by the disease that she had to walk with the aid of crutches. Rosa remembers that Montse looked a bit doubtful, but stayed to pitch in and help with hanging pictures. When she left she was cheerful and happy, "having lost that little doubt she had when she came in." Montse's mother recalls, "When she came home that night she was delighted with herself. I think her heart was stolen from her that very first day."

After that first visit, Montse began visiting Llar after school and on weekends. Many of the Opus Dei girls have vivid memories of her. Rosa comments: "She had a winning manner and was very lively.... She was tremendously spontaneous. She had many splendid human qualities." Another mentioned, "She was always cheerful and happy.... Right from the beginning, she understood that cheerfulness is a basic trait of the spirit of Opus Dei.... She was fun-loving and so bubbling with life and health that it was a joy to be by her side." Another remarked that Montse was "above all a sportswoman. She was always talking about her tennis matches, her mountain climbing, her friends ... and the theater, in which she occasionally participated as an actress." And she loved to sing, swim, cycle, ski, climb mountains, and play cards, tennis, basketball, and table tennis. She also loved to join in the *Sardanas*, a traditional festive circle dance.

From Montse's first association with Opus Dei, her mother noted, she began to change. She no longer protested when her brothers and sisters teased her about being a little overweight. Her little temper was controlled, and she began to make efforts to correct some character defects such as not complaining when she was called "Montsita," a name she disliked. She also began to mortify herself in little things — such as leaping out of bed when she awoke, in an effort not to yield to laziness. After school she would visit Llar, where she did her homework, engaged in a time of mental prayer, attended a formation class, and then helped with the chores of the center. On returning home, before helping her mother, she always greeted an image of Our Lady of Montserrat located at the end of a corridor. It is said that many of the customs of Christian living that Opus Dei taught her, she was already living, having learned them in her deeply pious home.

When Montse was fifteen, she wanted to become a nurse; but, as she was too young to begin studies, she enrolled in the professional school for women named L'Escola, where she studied domestic sciences, drawing, sewing, and crafts. The environment was not particularly appealing to Montse, since the girls were older and often engaged in unsuitable conversations. Despite this, she worked hard, went to Mass often, and continued to deepen her interior life.

Finally, after making a retreat, Montse asked Emilia ("Lia") Vila, the new director of Llar, for admission in Opus Dei. Lia remembers, "It was not a sentimental, momentary rapture, or a whim of the moment. Montse was a stable girl. She did not act on sudden impulse. It was a mature, meditated decision, and totally free. . . . Montse had a strong personality, not easily influenced. It (the calling) was from God."

That night while walking home from Llar, Montse "was bursting with joy." She had committed herself to God on Christmas Eve.

From then on, Lia remembers, Montse continued with her normal activities. Then one day following a ski trip, she and her friends started running home; after a short distance, Montse was forced to stop by an intense pain in her left leg. Some days later, when she continued to limp, Dr. Saenz was consulted, but attached no importance to it and prescribed vitamins. When the pain persisted, she was told to wear a knee-guard.

On days when the pain relented, she continued her visits at Llar where, Fr. Julia remembers, "Montse was just another one of the girls." She did not do anything extraordinary. She went to daily Mass, did half an hour of prayer in the mornings and another half an hour in the evenings; and, sometimes, she was seen to pray on her knees for the whole half hour. She offered her work before starting it and performed various services for others. She read the New Testament and other spiritual books regularly. She said all three parts of the Rosary and paid visits to the Blessed Sacrament.

The pain in her knee persisted, but when she could, she continued her sporting activities. This might have aggravated her condition, since she was finally obliged to visit a specialist who ordered X-rays. These showed a slight separation of the periosteum, but in 1958, the significance of this symptom was unknown. Another doctor was consulted; what one recommended, the other discouraged. Finally, a Dr. Martin ordered a series of X-rays that revealed a tumorous mass. On June 20, 1958, the diagnosis was confirmed: Montse had Ewing's sarcoma, a malignant and irreversible cancer of the bone.

The only treatment available at that time was radiation, so Montse started it. But this proved to be a trying experience even before she reached the hospital for the treatments, since her leg was so painful by this time that she could not suppress a grimace when walking or getting into or out of a taxi.

Whenever she could, she visited Llar, where Lia recalls her saying, "I am ready to put up with whatever comes. . . . I am very afraid of suffering and the doctors frighten me . . . but if God sends me more suffering, He will help me a lot."

On the day of her seventeenth birthday, July 10, her friends at Llar celebrated with games and songs. By this time they knew the gravity of Montse's illness, although Montse herself had not yet been told. Finally, she insisted, and her father told her what to expect. She accepted it well and was then seen kneeling before the image of Our Lady of Montserrat. During the night when her mother checked on her, she was again kneeling before Our Lady and was heard to say, "Whatever you want."

On her next visit to Llar, Lia noted that she seemed perfectly happy and was singing peacefully. Montse finally remarked to Lia, "I really am at peace. I want God's will. This is the second time I give myself to God. I have already done it once before." The pain, she said was a "purification to get to heaven."

One regret, however, broke her heart. She would not now become a member of Opus Dei, and would never be able to live at Llar in community, something she had eagerly anticipated.

One of her friends recalls: "The extraordinary part of Montse's behavior lay precisely in her normality. She had the ability to endure her illness without attracting attention to herself; she did not try to be the center of attention and gave no importance at all to her ailment. When we asked her about her illness she would respond without either exaggeration or frivolity.... She never wanted to be 'a special case,' though she could have been, considering that she was so young and, of all the girls who went to Llar, the only one who was ill."

Despite her illness, she performed in a play named *The House of Quiros,* in which she played the part of an aged housekeeper of a traditional Castillian manor house. One of her lines read: "This is not suitable for someone of my age! Oh Mother of Mercy, I am dying!" Because everyone attending knew of her condition, it is said that a sad shudder ran through the whole audience. Her mother remarked afterward, "I did not expect Montse to act so well or so naturally."

The play was a foretaste of her future, for it was after that performance that the pain worsened and never left her. She attended a celebration on October 2, the 30th anniversary of the foundation of Opus Dei, but was forced to leave quietly because of the pain.

Montse knew that her days were numbered, but one would never suspect she was so ill. She never complained and lived with such serenity one would think she had a long lifetime ahead of her. She seemed to be her former carefree and happy self, but occasionally those who knew her well could see on her face the pain she was suffering.

In November, the members of Opus Dei planned a trip to Rome and insisted that Montse join them. Since she would have companions to help her, she was delighted that she would be near the pPope and meet the founder of Opus Dei, the future St. Josemaria Escriva. The days in Rome were the happiest days of her life, in spite of the pain. She toured St. Peter's Basilica and the next day met with the holy founder. Escriva was told of her condition and had words of encouragement for her. He made the Sign of the Cross on her forehead, saying: "My daughter, sufferings you have and will have, but I want you to offer it up for your parents, your brothers and sisters, for the Work and for me. . . . Ask Our Lord for His will to be done, but that if He wishes, you can get better again. Promise me that from now on you will always be faithful." Afterward he gave the seventeen-year-old a look of deep love and affection.

During the trip, one of her friends reports, "She was happy with us, as if nothing were the matter. She had difficulty getting around, although she did not attract attention." Another friend recalls, "During Mass she made a special effort not to show her pain: she did not grimace or show any trace of frustration on her face. She stood up, the same as everyone else when the liturgy required, but she remained sitting because she could not kneel."

When asked if she was in serious pain, however, she replied, "Yes. It is as if a mad dog were biting me all the time."

In December, Montse spent more time in bed, praying, singing, playing card games, and talking with friends who came to visit. When Christmas was near, her sickroom was decorated for the occasion, with Montse directing the placement of each article. This activity was bittersweet, because she knew this Christmas would be her last one on earth.

During the Christmas season, through the influence of the Begian ambassador, Montse's father received an experimental drug from Russia he had heard about. With her doctor's approval, Montse consented to take the medication, but this caused a dreadful reaction with days of vomiting. Finally, Montse's mother asked her if she wanted to discontinue the medication. Always wanting to do the will of God, she asked her mother to decide for her. The treatment was discontinued.

One day when the family seemed very sad, Montse told them, "When I die, I don't want anyone to be sad. You must be cheerful."

From the middle of January on, it became increasingly painful for fresh dressings to be applied to her badly swollen leg. One can only imagine the pain when the inflammation burst. Sometimes when the old bandage was removed, bits of flesh would come off with it. Montse's mother recalls that it took four people to do the dressing. Two would hold up her leg while another applied gauze and the other the bandage. The procedure was very painful and delicate because of the large number of ulcers and the small hemorrhages that occurred.

To the amazement of all, Montse resisted taking sedatives or anything that would alleviate the pain. Her reason for this soon became evident: the medication would make her sleep and diminish her suffering, thereby interrupting the pain she was offering to Our Lord for the pope, for Opus Dei, the holy founder, her family, and others whom she mentioned.

Thankfully, her many friends visited her and prayed with her; one even taught her how to play the guitar. She continued to show consideration for others and always tried to look her best to leave them with a positive impression of her condition.

Everyone was now praying for her cure through the intercession of Isidoro Zorzano, a medical doctor who had been a member of Opus Dei. (His Cause for Beatification has also been introduced.) Often those in the sickroom read aloud the prayer on his holy card.

But the time finally came when even the sheet touching the leg was unbearable. A kind of cage was constructed so that it would not touch her. And every time her caregivers changed the dressing, a towel had to be placed beneath the leg to absorb the liquid that seeped from the wound.

Because her condition was worsening, she received the necessary dispensation for her definitive acceptance into Opus Dei, a ceremony that took place on February 5, 1959, with her family and friends from Llar in attendance. It is noted that Montse was "totally serene," but when everyone left, she dissolved into tears — both from happiness and from fatigue and pain. Even in such torment, however, she declined the use of a hospital adjustable bed that could have made her more comfortable. In addition, someone had given her a present of a pillow for her head. It proved to be very bothersome, but she insisted on using it to please the person who had given it to her. Those attending her could see that it was uncomfortable, but Montse tried to convince them that it suited her perfectly.

The priests of Opus Dei, as well as other priests, visited her every day bringing her the Holy Eucharist, but sometimes after a sleepless night she would doze off during her thanksgiving. She would be awakened as she had requested because, as she said, "Without the Eucharist I could not live."

We are told that she was always concerned about others and especially those who stayed with her at night, always asking if they were cold or needed something to drink. She was often heard whispering ejaculations and would follow those who recited the rosary with her.

Montse's father finally decided that it was time for her to receive the Sacrament of the Sick. Don Florencio came in the afternoon and, in the presence of her family and close friends, administered the sacrament. Afterward, she asked when it would all end, because "I am really looking forward to going . . ." When her mother said that perhaps Our Lord wished her to continue helping souls, Montse replied, "Then I don't mind a few more days, or whenever Our Lord wills." Toward the end she was heard to repeat, "Whenever you like, wherever you like, as you like."

Then came the day when she told her mother, "Mom, how hard these little things are!" When asked what little things, Montse pointed to her mouth. She was suffering a horrible thirst. She could not drink anything because then she could not breathe. She suffered this discomfort as Our Lord suffered it on the Cross, in compliance with the will of God.

As she repeated the name "Jesus," she clutched at her crucifix and died on Holy Thursday, March 26, 1959. She had suffered her agony and joined Our Lord to enter her heavenly reward on the eve of Good Friday.

Almost immediately, she was honored as a saint, with requests for prayer cards and biographies coming from around the world. Testimonials of favors received through her intercession were forthcoming and the first steps toward her beatification were begun three years after her death. The Congregation for the Causes of Saints issued the decree declaring the validity of the process on May 15, 1992. As part of the process, her remains were exhumed for identification and were transferred to the Bonaigua Residence Hall in Barcelona. There, she has many visitors, including her beloved members of Opus Dei. ✝

Venerable Paula Renata Carboni

1908 – 1927
19 years old
ITALY

$\mathcal{P}$aula was born in Montefalcone Appennino, in the diocese of Fermo, on February 21, 1908, the fourth of eight children. Her father, a surgeon, was upright and honest but hostile to religion of any sort, especially to Catholicism. His wife — perhaps to maintain peace in the family — complied with his beliefs and instructed her children accordingly. They were forbidden to enter a church or talk to a priest, and the father demanded that his orders be respected.

Thus, during her childhood the family never spoke of God. However, the family did not know that Paula's aunt, Giuseppina Majeski, had Paula secretly baptized when she was very young. She also taught Paula the first elements of the Catechism.

When the family moved to Grottazzolina, Paula continued her studies, but was later sent to another school in Fermo with her sister, Giuseppina. This proved to be providential, since they lived near a pious Catholic family named Maricotti. Here, for the first time, the two girls were enveloped in a Christian atmosphere where they started to know God, study the Catechism, and frequent the parish church. Paula was then fourteen years old. Together with her sister Giuseppina, they were instructed by the parish priest, received Holy Communion, and were confirmed by Bishop Charles Castelli . . . all without their father's knowledge. But one day, probably summoning all the courage they could muster and with "steadiness and sweetness," they revealed their secret to their father. Unable to change their views, he left them to follow a faith he detested.

A great influence in Paula's spiritual progress was the book, *History of a Soul*, written by St. Thérèse of Lisieux. Paula began reading this book at the time of her first Holy Communion, and she continued to use it for her meditations until the time of her death. She was so drawn to the saint and her book that Paula began to imitate the saint, hoping to become a perfect copy of her.

From the age of thirteen, Paula suffered from a form of colic that often forced her to bed, but she considered this illness as a precious gift of the Lord. In addition to this ailment, she looked for occasions to mortify herself and rejoiced when she could offer some cross as an expression of her love of Jesus. She eventually wanted to totally devote herself to God and looked forward to becoming a missionary. Her bodily condition, however, would prevent this. Nevertheless, she offered herself to God for the conversion of sinners.

Applying herself to her studies, she received a teacher's diploma and taught for two years in the school of St. Clare in Fermo. She enrolled in Catholic Action and was distinguished for her ardor and her initiatives. She became diocesan secretary of the Female Youth, an office she administered with zeal and diligence. Of a tender age herself, she was still approached by many younger girls and helped them in their search for God. Her faith, love, supernatural wisdom, and mature mind attracted many of the young to her great heart, since she knew how to help the girls with their problems and to give wise directives and spiritual comfort.

During the Easter holidays of 1927, she and her sister pilgrimaged to Rome where they visited the places once visited by St. Thérèse. They prayed at the Coliseum and heard, and even touched, the Holy Father. Afterward, Paula said to a friend, "All is finished." She completed her total consecration to the love of God by making a vow of virginity on May 21, 1927. She was then nineteen years old.

During August of the same year, while she was at Grottazzolina and still enduring a problem with indigestion, she contracted typhus and a very high fever. Much to the dismay of her relatives — especially her father, who was helpless to stop her suffering — Paula remained peaceful and was happy to complete her immolation as a victim to the love of God. She offered her sufferings for the conversion of sinners, but especially for her father, that he would convert to God.

Knowing she was about to die, she asked to see her confessor. Although her father tried to change her mind, she insisted, and died a very holy death on September 11, 1927.

Paula Renata Carboni had a brief existence, but her soul was endowed with a rich spiritual life that touched the heights of union with God in true Christian charity.

The funeral was held in the parish church, but the father, faithful to his principles, refused to enter the building. On the way to the cemetery, however, he did accompany the remains and, while looking at the casket as it was placed in the grave, remarked, "Now she is with her God."

Paula's prayers for her father's conversion were answered some years later, when he accepted God and the Catholic faith.

The informative process for the beatification of Paula Renata Carboni was begun in 1951. In 1965, the remains were exhumed and entombed in the Church of the Madonna of Mercy in Fermo. Paula was declared Venerable in 1993. ✝

Servant of God Rachelina Ambrosini

1925 – 1941
15 years old
ITALY

The spirituality of this young girl was so highly regarded by everyone who came in contact with her that she was called "the girl who lived for heaven."

She was born in Venticano, Italy, on July 2, 1925, to Alberto and Filomena Sordillo, who provided their daughter with an excellent Christian education. They were careful to instill in her a love of the faith and devotion to all that pertained to the Church, as well as a dedication to duty.

Rachelina was described as being obedient, docile, of a vivacious nature, and extremely intelligent. At the age of seven, she received the Eucharist for the first time with great devotion, a characteristic that developed steadily throughout her short life.

During the time she attended the primary school, she contracted a bad case of measles, but otherwise pursued her studies without incident. She became a boarder at the Institute of St. Rose in Bari, where she was under the care of a priestly uncle who was also the headmaster of the school. When she was only eleven years old, her father became seriously ill with little hope of recovery. Rachel prayed fervently for him and even offered her life to God in exchange for that of her father. (Apparently, his health improved, as he was later called to arms for the war declared by Mussolini and Hitler.)She completed her studies with honors and earned the respect and love of the students, teachers, and all who knew her.

After completing her studies in Bari, she transferred to Rome in 1940 to continue her education as a boarder at the Liceo Cabrini (the College of St. Francesca Saverio Cabrini), conducted by Saint Frances Cabrini's missionary nuns. Here she distinguished herself as a diligent student, a kind and understanding friend, and a ready assistant to all who needed help, especially to the poor and the weak. She was noted for her filial respect toward the nuns, her love of the church, and her devout reception of the sacraments.

Through correspondence with her priestly uncle, she was carefully guided in the spiritual life and is said to have reached the heights of Christian perfection.

When her health began to decline in 1941, she was diagnosed with having purulent otitis, a severe infection of the ear. Unattended for a time, the infection spread, caused severe pain, and became life threatening. But even as her sickness progressed, no one believed the fifteen-year-old would die; on the other hand, she insisted with certainty that she would die, even predicting the date.

Finally, it seemed that she would indeed succumb to the disease, and she received the Sacrament of the Sick from the hospital chaplain. Even in her exhausted state she was still able to receive the sacrament with transports of joy and gratitude, a condition that inspired all those present to tears. After administering the sacrament, the chaplain turned to those in attendance and said in all certitude, "She is an angel, not of this earth." Just as she had predicted, she entered heaven on March 10, 1941.

The saintly teenager's body was taken back to her native city to be buried in the chapel of the local cemetery, where those who loved her as the "Lily of Irpinia" attended the service. Later, in 1958, her remains were entombed in the parish church of Venticano where her grave was the destination of devotees who demonstrated the trust they had in her intercession by offering countless prayers to her.

Finally, in 1959, the Archbishop of Benevento began the informative process for her beatification. Completed in 1991, the decree for her beatification was accepted by the Congregation for the Cause of the Saints in 1995. ✝

Ramon Montero Navarro

1931 – 1945
13 years old
SPAIN

*R*amon was born in La Mancha, Spain, in the area made famous by Cervantes and his knight, Don Quixote. He was born into a very devout Catholic family at a time when the faith was being greatly tested. Communist forces were gathering momentum: priests and religious were persecuted and often killed, sacred objects were burned in the town square, churches were being vandalized or even destroyed (such as the one in the village of Tomelloso). Because of this chaos, Ramon's First Communion was delayed, but the family continued all their spiritual activities.

The father, Elias Montero, was a clerk in a clothing store, but he returned to the land he loved to tend his vineyards. He was outstanding for his piety — in an era when most men felt religion was the domain of women — and gathered the family together each evening for the recitation of the rosary. Both parents also attended daily Mass. Victoria, Ramon's mother, was a devotee of Our Lady of Mount Carmel and of the scapular, a devotion she instilled in her children.

Her efforts bore fruit; one son became a priest, another is being considered for beatification.

As for Ramon, he was an ordinary young boy who enjoyed games and sports and was particularly fond of his favorite soccer team, Bilboa Athletic. He was prepared for his First Communion by the Sisters of Charity. Because their church had been destroyed, the sisters allowed Ramon, his sister, Maruja, and other youngsters to receive Our Lord for the first time in the patio of the convent. After the service, Ramon's mother asked him if he had requested many things of Our Lord. His answer was astounding: "I asked the Lord to make me like the beloved disciple. Let Him send me suffering; let Him send me whatever he wants. I want to offer myself up for you, for sinners, for everybody. But let him send me much suffering, so that He lives in me like in his beloved disciple."

The beloved disciple was St. John, as the mother was later to learn from Sr. Felices, a Vincentian nun who sometimes stopped to visit Mrs. Montero. For her part, Sr. Felices said she looked at the boy and thought to herself, "This is an angel."

The nuns' confessor, Fr. José Tomas, helped Ramon spiritually as well. Fr. José once confided to the parents, "I come away from his confessions amazed. He makes his confession like an adult, with a great sense of responsibility."

The suffering Ramon asked for at the time of his first Holy Communion soon came to pass. He and his family lived in the country by their vineyards during the unrest of the Spanish Civil War, and the children of the area delighted in taking rides on a mule. One day, while Ramon was riding it, the mule reared up, throwing him to the ground. He landed on his back and was speechless for more than half an hour. As his mother massaged the area, she noticed that the vertebrae were not in alignment and quickly consulted a specialist, who prescribed a corset-like bandage. Soon an abscess developed on Ramon's back. The corset-like bandage was then exchanged for a plaster cast, which caused even more difficulties.

To relieve open sores that developed on Ramon's body, his doctor recommended he lie on his stomach; this provided only partial relief. When Ramon saw five sores on his body, he likened these to the five wounds of Our Lord.

Upon more careful examination, the doctor diagnosed Ramon with Pott's disease, a degeneration of the vertebral bones. The St. John of God brothers, who minister to the sick, told his parents that the disease is so painful that often they had to tie children with this disease to their beds; otherwise, they would attempt to end their lives to escape the pain.

Ramon, on the other hand, bravely announced that doctors were unnecessary since Jesus assisted him, and he wanted to accept whatever the Lord sent him. On days when the pain was almost unbearable, he would ask to see the picture of Spain's patroness, the Virgen del Pilar, and request family members to gather near him to recite the rosary. Without fail, at the third decade, Ramon would announce that he felt much relieved.

But just as he was able to cope with the complications of Pott's disease, Ramon was diagnosed with a kidney stone. Doctors prescribed morphine, but Ramon refused to accept it and pleaded with his mother not to force him to take it. The doctor insisted it was inhuman to permit the boy to suffer such atrocious pain; even the St. John of God brothers agreed, but Ramon insisted on suffering what the Lord had given him.

Seeing the anxiety his parents suffered, Ramon attempted to console them. He once told his mother during Holy Week, "Mom, when you are deeply hurt because your son suffers so much, place the Blessed Virgin in front of you, and tell the Virgin: 'Who am I, my Mother, not to suffer what you suffered?' And she was the Blessed Virgin! Nothing less than the Mother of God! Just remember that and you will see how consoled you will be."

Despite Ramon's desire for suffering, however, his family fervently prayed for a cure.

The town priests told visiting priests about Ramon, and they in turn came to see the youngster. One such priestly visitor engaged in conversation with Ramon at such length that he forgot an appointment and was reminded only when altar boys came in search of him. When he asked Ramon's parents where the boy had learned his religion, he was told that Ramon's only instructions had been in preparation for his first Holy Communion. At that, the priest left, fully convinced that Ramon was enlightened by the Holy Spirit.

Soon many people, even clergy, were appealing to Ramon for prayers. Many of these requests were answered — and verified by priests who witnessed them.

With the early onset of his illness, Ramon's formal education was limited, but he managed to advance on his own. He kept a detailed diary of the happenings in his home and the village, even to giving the scores of the games involving his favorite soccer team. In addition, he was aware of everything happening around his house. Once, when his mother saw a poor little boy around Ramon's age, she gave him something to eat and a change of Ramon's clothing. Ramon asked her to find the boy again and give him a second set of clothes, saying, "You should have given him another change of clothing, because when he changes, what will he wear?" The family was amazed when, following this incident, an aunt from Madrid arrived with clothing for Ramon exactly like the clothes given to the beggar boy.

When the Carmelite friars moved to the area, they began to visit Ramon on a daily basis, bringing him Holy Communion and supplying him with spiritual reading. Almost a third of Ramon's diary is devoted to these good prelates. Ramon dearly loved Our Lady of Mount Carmel and asked the Carmelites if he could become part of their religious family. At that time there were no male members of the local Third Order, but Father Pedro petitioned for a dispensation and was able to clothe Ramon in the habit of a tertiary. Ramon was taught to pray the Little Office of Our Lady of Mt. Carmel and was instructed on the obligations of a Carmelite tertiary. The day of his profession was observed as a solemn feast, with the family picture of Our Lady of Mount Carmel prominently displayed.

While everyone who knew of Ramon's illness marveled at his patience while suffering a disease that would ordinarily bring one to contemplate suicide, Ramon wrote in his diary:

> When you ask for something you do not look down on it. I asked for suffering for sinners, and for patience to put up with the pain. How good Our Blessed Mother of Carmel has been! She granted me both things.

On the feast day of Our Lady of Mount Carmel, July 16, 1942, Ramon somehow gathered the energy to attend services in the church. Afterward his health began to deteriorate rapidly. He realized on his own that, humanly speaking, the pain he experienced was unbearable, yet he credited the Blessed Mother for giving him the grace to endure it. With wisdom beyond his age, he would explain, "How could I turn my back on this grace when I asked for it in the first place?" His serenity, cheerfulness, alertness, and kindness left people in wonder. One of these visitors, a Carmelite Fr. Ismael Martinez, exclaimed, "I've never seen an angel, but I think that if one did take flesh, he'd have to be something like Ramon." When the Carmelites commissioned the sculptor Rafael Barbero of Seville to create a statue of Our Lady of Mount Carmel, they asked him to fashion the face of the Child Jesus to resemble Ramon, so that his image would always remain with them.

Ramon's pain increased to the point where he spent many sleepless nights in prayer, yet he persevered in cheerfulness. Although he did not speak of death, but only of the beauty of heaven, he mentioned February 1 to his father in an offhand manner that made his father wonder about its meaning.

Upon seeing his mother suffering anxiety over his condition, Ramon told her in all simplicity, "Everything you are suffering on my account, if you will put up with it with patience and joy, you too will earn a very good place in heaven. The same goes for Dad. All of you who are suffering, although Dad accepts it with more patience than you, you shouldn't suffer so much for seeing me this way...."

It was snowing on February 1, 1945, as Ramon waited for the Holy Eucharist to be brought to him. "When they bring me Holy Communion," he said, "I don't want anything, not even water. Today I don't need anything. I don't even feel the pain." Around 11:30 he asked to see his father, who was surprised, since his son rarely called for him. To his question, "What can I do for you?" Ramon answered, "Nothing, I just wanted to see you." He then asked his mother to raise him up and hold him. With his eyes fixed on the crucifix, he died peacefully in his mother's arms as the church bells rang the midday Angelus.

Ramon was buried in the Carmelite Third Order habit, with the scapular of Our Lady of Mount Carmel on his chest and his often-recited rosary in his hands. He was only thirteen years old.

The investigation into the Cause for his Beatification has been initiated in his diocese. ✝

Santos Franco Sanchez

1942 – 1954
11 years old
SPAIN

$\mathcal{H}$e dreamed of entering the minor seminary of the Carmelite Order, but this devout schoolboy willingly sacrificed his long-held desire, accepted the will of God, and died of a painful illness when he was only eleven years old.

It is not surprising that he chose the Carmelite Order, since he attended the Carmelite school in Hinojosa del Duque, Spain, where Carmelite friars taught him. With the Carmelite presence, the area was said to be "thoroughly Carmelite," an area that gave many vocations to the order — including two of Santos' sisters, who became cloistered Carmelite nuns.

Santos was born July 6, 1942, at Hinojosa del Duque (Cordoba). The Carmelite influence in the area carried over into his home, as both parents were Carmelite tertiaries. Santos' father, Manuel, had a small shoe factory; his mother, Maria del Carmen, was a dedicated and loving housewife and mother. Of the thirteen children born to this religious couple, Santos was the sixth. Three children died in infancy.

The parents participated daily at an early Mass so that Manuel could arrive at work in time to prepare the assignments of his employees, and Maria del Carmen could arrive home in time to prepare the children for school and attend to her household chores. By all accounts they were ideal parents who gave their children a good example and who treated each of their children as unique gifts of God. They developed in the children a fervent and deep love for Jesus in the Eucharist and urged them to make frequent visits to the Blessed Sacrament. The Blessed Mother was not neglected in their formation, either; Maria del Carmen told her children that she had consecrated them to Our Lady of Mount Carmel while they were still in the womb.

Santos was a normal child who joined in noisy, unrestrained games with the youngsters who played in front of his home. But neighbors noticed Santos helped maintain peace between disagreeing playmates, and it was he who invariably took the side of the weaker companion. This desire for peace included members of his family as well, and he frequently settled disagreements between his brothers and sisters.

He was punctual and obedient in performing tasks assigned by his parents — although when the assignment seemed more suited to his sisters, he didn't mind calling this to their attention! He had the usual limitations of boys his age, but his goodness and charity far exceeded them.

We are indebted to Fr. Augustine Cobos, O.Carm., for giving us many testimonials of his holy pupil. Fr. Cobos taught Santos for two years and often visited him during his illnes. He described his memories of Santos in 1990:

He was a boy to whom you paid attention for his candor, his humility, his obedience, and for so many other qualities and for virtues which are not frequently found in youngsters his age. He was intelligent and studious, but this did not make him feel superior to others, On the contrary, when he gave the answer to something that the others had not known, you could see him blush as if ashamed of himself. He was a devout youngster. I frequently met him in our church in Hinojosa, making a visit to the Lord or participating in the Rosary. He went to confession to me on many occasions with so much devotion that if I hadn't known his devout parents, I would have been astounded.

Santos' health was excellent until the end of November 1953, when his right ear began to hurt. A discharge was noticed and he was brought to the doctor, who declared it a minor problem. The discharge stopped, but then was replaced by painful and constant headaches that actually prevented him from attending school. A second visit to the doctor, however, produced the same diagnosis — a simple cold that would go away in time.

When the pain grew worse, Santos told his mother, "My head hurts a lot, but the doctors say I don't have anything. Don't worry about it, Mom. Let what God wants be done."

During the month of December, his situation worsened with the presence of a fever. Although suffering, Santos showed no signs of irritation or impatience and accepted his condition as God's will for him.

Because their own doctor refused to see the seriousness of the boy's condition, the family decided to bring him to a young doctor whose specialty was eye, ear, and nose difficulties. This doctor indicated that since the ear was no longer festering, in his opinion, the headaches had nothing to do with an infection; he believed the problem was in the nervous system and prescribed a tranquilizer.

But the tranquilizers did no good; Santos grew steadily worse and began experiencing dizzy spells. Although he never complained, his pain was obvious in the strained expression on his face. He once confided, "This doctor does not believe me, either. He says that really my head does not ache. The Lord knows that it does ache, but I want His will to be done. Don't be concerned for me. I am offering up everything to the Lord."

Since two doctors were unable to properly diagnose the patient's condition, Santos' father, Manuel, consulted a third doctor, a retired friend of his, who hurried to the Franco house. He took little time in reaching a definite diagnosis: Santos was suffering from meningitis. He urged the parents to take the boy to Cordoba for immediate attention. At last someone believed in the seriousness of the boy's condition.

At Cordoba, however, the family was given sad news. Over the period of time wasted with others' misdiagnoses, Santos' infection had spread to the brain and become terminal; little could be done even to alleviate the pressure and pain. After complaining about his colleagues in Hinojosa who had failed to take Santos' condition seriously, the specialist made an incision behind the boy's ear to drain some of the infected material.

Accompanying Santos and his mother to the hospital was a priest friend, Don Juan Jurado. He suggested their sufferings be offered for the Church and the missions. But Santos was a few steps ahead of him, replying, "From the first moment that I began to experience pain, I haven't stopped offering everything to the Lord for all those intentions . . . and also for sinners." Both the priest and the hospital staff were edified and amazed by the serenity of the young patient.

After Santos returned home, a priest was called to anoint him and bring him Holy Communion. Surrounded by his family, Santos attentively followed the last rites; afterward, he softly said to his mother, "Mom, let them leave me alone so that I can make my thanksgiving. But you stay with me to help me."

During his illness, Santos was very pleasant with his brothers and sisters and, despite his suffering, tried to keep a smiling face. But once, when the pain was especially severe, he appealed to his mother, "Tell the youngsters not to yell so much. I cannot put up with the pain. But don't tell Dad; he will suffer too much. I want God's will to be fulfilled. I offer up everything to Him for sinners, for the missions, and for everything God wishes."

Soon, Santos was so weak he could speak only in a very soft voice. But during prayer, he was heard to say, "My God, take me to heaven. I'm too small to suffer so much. However, Your will be done. Everything just as You will it. I offer it to You for sinners, for the missions."

Periodic convulsions racked his poor emaciated body while he writhed in pain. His sufferings, reflected on his face, were so severe that the helpless parents worried their child would lose his mind. After one of the convulsions, while he lay still as a corpse, the family checked his pulse to see if he were still alive. Aware of this, Santos assured them, "No, not yet. I still have more to suffer. God only knows when I'll go to heaven. I offer everything to Him." Sometimes, Santos said he was offering his sufferings for children.

His devotion to Our Lady was that of a loving child, and he was often heard to pray, "Help me, you who are my mother. I'm very little; don't leave me. Yes, my heavenly mother is here." Of his earthly mother he asked, "Pray the rosary, but slowly so that I can follow."

His prayers to Jesus were frequent, once softly commenting, "You suffered more than this on the cross, and when they crowned You with thorns, Your head ached very much."

One day when he seemed to have regained a little strength, he asked his father to assemble the family beside him. He then bid farewell to each of them and embraced them one by one and said a little something to each of them. He then revealed, "Soon, I'm going to heaven. I have very little time left. I will not forget you. I love you very much. Don't cry, because I'm happy. What do sufferings matter?"

Santos particularly prayed to Our Lady of Mount Carmel and made touching comments about her. He even announced that she had visited him, and after describing her, he commented, "Mother, how I love you." His earthly mother thought he was speaking to her, but he corrected her, "I am saying it to my Blessed Mother, the Virgin, who is right here."

Another time he described the Child Jesus, coming with a host of angels. Santos even said that he received a crown consisting of white and red flowers. His mother suggested that the crown was a symbol of his soul, which was white. "But the red flowers indicate that you are still called to suffer a little more," she added, "so that your soul will be even more pure."

As the painful days passed slowly, his schoolmates visited him in small groups. Santos smiled at them as they stood by the door. They noted the large bandage on his head that protected the drainage from his ear, and the crucifix that he held atop his chest.

The Carmelite friars frequently visited him as well, especially Fr. Cobos. Santos' doctor also paid a visit every morning. A professed atheist, nevertheless he admired the prayerful attitude of his young patient. Santos once told the doctor, "Do you know why I can suffer so much? Because God is with me." On another occasion he told the doctor about the Blessed Virgin's visits to him. He also spoke of his guardian angel protecting him and giving him strength. The doctor admitted, "This child has something special about him; if I didn't see him myself, I wouldn't believe it."

One of his sisters, now a Carmelite nun, was by his bedside one day when she saw her brother suddenly sit up in bed and shout while holding his crucifix before him, "Get out of here, get out of here, ugly one. Look upon the cross of Christ crucified. Get out of here, ugly one." He then fell back on his pillow and resumed his normally quiet and immobile attitude. When the parents rushed to see what was happening, Santos announced clearly, "It was the devil, but he was scared away by the cross. He can do nothing against it."

Finally the last day arrived, February 6. When the noon Angelus bell sounded, he prayed aloud, "Take me, take me up to heaven, my Mother." After his sister prayed with him a favorite prayer to Our Lady, he said his last words, "God's will be done." He sighed deeply and died. It was the First Saturday of the month, a day dedicated to the Blessed Mother.

Father Cobos, who had visited Santos on the day of his death, gives us this impression of his former pupil:

When he fell ill and I found out about it, I went to see him. This made him happy. The first time I tried to encourage him I told him that he would soon be better and that he would be able to return to school again, but afterwards, seeing the conformity with which he accepted the will of God . . . I came home edified by his manner of speaking. He was offering his suffering for sinners and for vocations because his desire was to become a Carmelite Marianus (a seminarian). At the beginning of class on Monday, following his death, we prayed to the Lord for his soul and I said to his school companions, "Surely he is in heaven. God wished to purify him by means of his painful sickness, which he accepted with authentic faith because he loved the Lord very much."

The Cause for Santos' eventual Beatification has been entrusted to the Carmelite Order. +

Servant of God Silvio Dissegna

1967 – 1979
12 years old
ITALY

$\mathcal{A}$lthough Silvio was born in Moncalieri near Turin on July 1, 1967, his parents, Ottavio and Gabriella Dissegna, actually lived in the village of Poirino, where they were regarded as an exemplary family. They were extremely proud and happy with the birth and had Silvio baptized in the hospital chapel five days later. This outstanding couple provided Silvio and his brother Carlo with a thorough Christian education and a good family environment that fostered a deep love of the faith.

From his earliest years, Silvio demonstrated a lively intelligence and a love of all the usual activities of his age. When it was time for him to attend school in 1973, he went eagerly and never complained. Healthy and vivacious, he liked to play ball, take rides on his bicycle, and watch television cartoons. He was a popular boy, known for his pleasant smile, and had a special concern for his fellow students, especially during games. As one fellow student wrote, "He played with joy, but if someone was hurt, he withdrew from the game in order to take care of him. If it was not a serious condition, he would continue to play."

His interest in all things religious began early, especially after he received his first Holy Communion on September 7, 1975. He was faithful to his prayers and the study of the Catechism and was often found reading the Gospels and other religious books. It was evident that he had an intense relationship with Jesus; concerned about pleasing Him, Silvio faithfully performed the little duties assigned to him by his parents. He had a charming character and a marvelous sensibility for others. "I want my actions to be good," he would say. "I want to pray with joy and to help those in need, respecting all."

One day in 1977, when his mother was cleaning his room, she found a piece of paper in his typewriter which read, "Beloved Mother, I thank you for putting me in the world, to have given me a life that is so beautiful. I want to live a long time."

Unfortunately, a long life was not to be his. At the beginning of the next year, Silvio experienced a persistent pain in his left leg. Several doctor visits and various medications followed, but nothing seemed to help. Finally he was taken to the hospital in Moncalieri where the condition was quickly seen as critical. Silvio apparently was aware from the beginning that his condition was terminal, and thus was not shocked when the family received the sad verdict: bone cancer. When his father was disconsolate at the verdict that the case was hopeless, Silvio consoled him: "Papa, have courage. Jesus will not abandon us. Papa, I will pray for you. I also need Jesus in order to be brave."

It was evident from then on, as a result of many prayers, rosaries, and the frequent reception of the Holy Eucharist, that God was guiding this youngster to a remarkable degree of sanctity. Silvio always yearned for his next Communion and often kissed a small statue of the Madonna. To his mother he once remarked, "If I die, it is not important. I will suffer to the end. Mother, we will be happy and content only in Paradise."

He frequently commented that he joined his pain to that of Jesus Crucified for the salvation of sinners. He often remarked, "Today I offer my suffering for the pope and the Church." Another day he would say, "Today I offer for the clergymen." And again, "Today I offer my pain for the conversion of sinners." His parish priest once declared, "Silvio, above all, offered his sufferings for the missions and for missionaries." He always held in his hands what he knew to be a mission rosary (also known as a Millennium rosary), with each decade of a different color.

As much as he could, Silvio continued his studies at home and even received the sacrament of Confirmation with his companions in the parish church of Poirino on June 4, 1978. Much to the edification of his schoolmates, Silvio attended the ceremony in a wheelchair.

From June until his death, Silvio was in and out of the hospital seven times and was even brought to Parish, where his parents hoped for a cure. The doctors, however, found the condition serious and began chemotherapy.

In the midst of so many suffering people in the hospital, Silvio revealed an exemplary faith and an unbelievable Christian fortitude. He requested Holy Communion every day and was serene in his suffering. The one concern that affected him a great deal was the swearing that he heard, especially words against the Madonna. Silvio promised that he would pray for the man responsible for this, even when he returned home.

During his last painful days he often remarked, "My vocation is to suffer. . . . I offer my pains to those of Jesus Crucified, for the entire humanity. . . . I must remain with Jesus, the one I have in my heart. Jesus, I suffer like when You were crucified. I join my sufferings to yours. . . . Every pain is a sign of love for You, my Jesus. . . ." He once said to his mother, "Mother, I am covering the road of Calvary and afterward there will be the crucifixion. . . . Jesus wants from me many sufferings and prayers."

The cancer devouring his leg, unfortunately, progressed throughout his body until he became blind in June and deaf in September. His acceptance of these conditions was extraordinary. He once confessed to his mother, "It is not so bad not seeing the sun, the light, the plants, the flowers, but it is hard not to see you, Papa, and Carlo." When the pain kept him awake, Silvio would recite fifteen mysteries of the Rosary, looking forward eagerly to the next morning's reception of the Holy Eucharist.

At last, Silvio's sufferings ended on September 24, 1979, after he received the Sacrament of the Sick, and he died with an angelic smile on his face. Two days later, his funeral was conducted in the parish church of Poirino. Attending were countless people of all ranks and a large number of priests. When the parish priest, Don Vincenzo Pensa, was asked how many clergymen participated, he replied, "How many? Thirty, forty . . . it is amazing that Silvio was known among so many clergymen."

Silvio's holiness was recognized quickly; the diocesan process for his canonization began the next February. It ended in October 2001, when Cardinal Severino Poletto, Archbishop of Turin, signed the official documents. These were then presented to the Congregation of the Causes of Saints.

Two biographies of the youngster were soon published: *To Die of Cancer at 12 Years of Age*, and *A Giant of 12 Years, Silvio*. Both books and others have spread the story of Silvio's courage beyond his little village to many parts of the world. As a result, Silvio has been the object of countless prayers of intercession. especially for the relief of suffering among the young.

When Cardinal Peter Palazzini, Prefect of the Congregation of the Causes of Saints, read one of these biographies, he wrote, "The example of Silvio illustrates that children are able to attain heroic virtues and are worthy of canonization."

The late Pope John Paul II, after reading the documents relative to the Cause, exclaimed, "Silvio is a beautiful example of an innocent soul who willingly endured pain for the love of God. We entrust his Cause to the Madonna." ✛

Servant of God Stephen Kaszap

1916 – 1935
19 years old
HUNGARY

Born into a pious and loving home, Stephen Kaszap was the third of five children. His father, a quiet, modest man, was chief supervisor at the local post office; his mother was an affectionate woman and a devoted homemaker. Both parents were concerned for the religious education of their children and taught them basic prayers at an early age. Family prayers were held each evening and — as was then the custom in Székesfehérvar, Hungary — during their Sunday Mass, the Kaszap family occupied the same family pew, near the pulpit in the local church.

As a child, Stephen was obstinate, aggressive, and indulged in fits of bad temper, even throwing objects when irritated or teased by his brothers. Even after he entered a school conducted by Cistercian monks, he took part in high-spirited antics and student mischief, though, as he wrote in his journal: "In general, I was quite willful and sometimes worked around the rules, but I was not perverted or corrupt. I have no doubt at all that I often irritated and annoyed the teachers…." (To his credit, he also had another side and could be happy and cooperative with daily chores.)

The good monks won out in the end, and Stephen's character began to show the qualities that would blossom in virtue to the end of his life. During these years, his journal gives good insights into his character and spiritual progress. He wrote that he made it a custom to rise promptly every morning, a custom that he continued for the rest of his life. He also noted that he served Holy Mass and "shall serve every day that I can."

He joined many of his comrades in the Congregation of Mary, whose main purpose was to increase their devotion and love of the Blessed Mother and to spread devotion to her. While still in school at Lycée, Stephen also joined the Boy Scouts. In his journal he wrote that a Boy Scout "should be an example in everything. He is never rude nor silly, but earnest and manly; at the same time, he is always joyful."

Some 60 years later, his patrol leader recollected some details from the days when Steven was a Boy Scout. He wrote: "During the three years I was patrol leader, there was never any discord between us. Whatever I asked, he carried out without argument or excuse. I could always trust him completely and always count on his support." This patrol leader, Ferenc Almassy, also reports, "Steve got up every morning earlier than the others to go to the edge of the forest to pray." The camp commander, a priest, relates that Steve was always at the morning Mass before returning to wait for the others to rise.

Stephen loved the outdoors and purchased a bicycle during the summer before his junior year so that he could take bike trips and explore forest lanes. He wrote that after reaching the Vértes Mountain, he roamed "its thick oak forests and its moss-strewn precipices where everything speaks about our Almighty Creator."

At this time, his journal began to grow larger to reveal many interests: notes on musical compositions and composers, including Mozart and Verdi; quotations from the writings of various well-known authors; and notes about painters and their paintings. He also began studying French, Italian, and Spanish, becoming so adept that he was able to serve as translator for Italian students visiting Hungary. His extracurricular interests at times overshadowed his schoolwork, to the point where his grades slipped and he had to revise his work schedule to correct the situation. The changes worked: by his graduation, he had a straight-A average. In his journal he wrote, "It was God's voice that guided me in my studies and helped me to carry them out with dedication."

Intellectual pursuits were not his only interests. He was also a gymnast, having joined his school team a year or so before graduation. In this, too, he excelled, winning a number of honors including several gold medals.

Before his eighteenth year, this candidate for eventual canonization had become a person of broad interests and a much-liked and respected member of his community. Graduating with distinction, he had served as student vice-president, a secretary of the Marian Congregation, and a scoutmaster. He'd even become a gymnastics champion. But what direction would his life take after graduation?

Stephen felt called to the religious life, but did not think himself capable of being a priest; he thought instead of becoming an elementary school teacher or, perhaps, a monk. His spiritual director, however, guided him toward the holy priesthood — the direction in which he believed God was calling Stephen. A retreat directed by a Carmelite priest confirmed the decision.

So, shortly after graduation, Stephen entered the Jesuit novitiate at the Hungarian Manresa House on July 30, 1934. Despite the "extraordinary heat" that sometimes gave him a headache, he wrote in his journal:

My Lord, how glad I am that You led me to such an excellent company. I see my colleagues' zeal and joyful devotion. My God, give me energy that I might resemble them . . . the greatest treasure on earth is the priestly life. We have given everything away, we have left everything behind, and now we must give our whole being.

In further entries, he also wrote:

The duty of the novice is to transform his soul in the spirit of the rule — leaving all work and worry aside in order to grow in spiritual life and in the practice of virtues. At every ringing of the bell think of obedience, let it be brisk, prompt, cheerful as if Jesus Christ himself were commanding or ordering.

One of his fellow novices once wrote of him, "The will of God always held him captive, making him always peaceful and smiling, and his whole personality reflected a well-balanced, pleasant individual."

After a 30-day retreat, his spiritual life blossomed so that almost all the future entries in his journal bore witness to his determination to increase in virtue and in the love of God. In the journal he admonishes himself for various faults, makes determined efforts to improve his meditations, plans to pray to the Holy Spirit every day for guidance, devises a program of self-denial and constant prayer, writes about the magnificence of the Holy Eucharist, and appeals to the saints for their prayers, especially those of the Blessed Mother and St. Joseph. By all appearances, he was a very determined novice who wanted most of all to comply with the will of God.

When Stephen entered the novitiate, he appeared to be in excellent health. The very next day, however, he became hoarse and soon lost his voice. His tonsils needed medical attention; then, soon after Christmas, his ankles became swollen with arthritic pain so that he could barely walk. Abscesses formed on his fingers, then on his neck and face. Tonsillitis reappeared. His torments must have been severe, since he wrote in his journal, "Any cross God gives must be carried with joy. . . . A little illness is more useful than ten or twenty years spent in health. . . . I suffer gladly for Christ and I don't run from pain."

In addition to these ailments, he suffered pleurisy, a high fever, and a nosebleed so severe it was nearly fatal. The bleeding vein had to be cauterized, adding to his suffering — as did more abscesses, which developed on his thighs and loins.

Surgery was scheduled for March 19, the feast of St. Joseph. After the operation, he whispered to his novice master, Fr. Hemm, "Holy Communion helped me greatly today and that is why I was so calm going in for surgery. I trust St. Joseph very much. . . . How small our sufferings are and how much the Church needs them. These thoughts make suffering much easier for me."

After his visit, his novice master reported to the other novices, "God's grace is marvelous. Brother Kaszap grows more in his spiritual life in one hour than we do in one year."

As soon as he could leave his bed, Stephen began to help his fellow patients and apparently spoke to them about the blessings of receiving Holy Communion. His influence was most noticeable at the Easter Holy Communion, when ten out of the eleven patients in his hospital ward received the Lord well prepared and with deep faith. The eleventh patient, a non-Catholic, exclaimed, "I never thought there was so much faith, harmony, and love in the Catholic faith [sic]."

For a time, Stephen's ailments would disappear, only to return with greater vigor. Although he was enthusiastic to resume his studies for the priesthood, it became apparent that his health wouldn't allow him to do so, and the day he left the novitiate was the saddest of his entire life. His colleagues gathered in the common room where each said a sad farewell.With a heavy heart, Stephen dressed once more in civilian clothes and took with him his large rosary and the cross he had been given when he received his cassock. Even as Stephen left, the Reverend Father Superior assured him that he could return when his health was firmly established, but he accepted his disappointment as the will of God: "Bodily sufferings cannot be compared to those of the soul," he wrote in his journal. "My whole life should be a continuous 'yes' to God."

A few days afterward, he was again admitted to the hospital, where he was diagnosed with erysipelas. After two weeks he returned home, attended church every morning, and, for the most part, continued the schedule of prayer and study he had practiced in the novitiate. But weeks later he was back in the hospital for the removal of his tonsils. This caused several hemorrhages and afterward, when the incision failed to heal properly, he was diagnosed with a tumor in the throat. His breathing became difficult and painful and, unable to speak, Stephen communicated by writing on a pad, asking for what he needed.

He asked most insistently for a priest and the last sacraments, but the nurse did not suspect that he was dying, and the priest was not notified.

Stephen's last notation, found after he expired, was this: "God be with you! We will meet in Heaven! Do not weep, this is my birthday in Heaven. God bless you all!" The date was December 17, 1935. He died holding the cross and a Marian medal and, finally — only after his death — received the Sacrament of the Sick and the papal blessing. He was just nineteen years old.

The bishop of Székesfehérvar, Msgr. Lajos Shvoy, initiated the Cause for Beatification seven years later, in October 1941. In 1942, the remains of Stephen Kaszap were carried in a triumphal procession to his present resting place, in a chapel of the Prohaszka Memorial Church.

Stephen Kaszap's name and reputation are well known not only in Hungary but in numerous other countries, where his biographies are popular. Many have appealed for his intercession, and many healings have resulted. +

Venerable Zeffirino (Ceffirino) Namuncura

—⚭—

1886 – 1905
19 years old
ARGENTINA

*A*t the end of the nineteenth and beginning of the twentieth centuries, European colonists gradually pushed into the farmlands of the Araucano Indians in Argentina, fencing off the best pastureland, setting up homesteads, and taking unfair advantage of the natives in every conceivable way. With only long spears as their weapons, the Indians were helpless against guns and charging cavalry troops.

To organize their resistance, the Indians chose as their chief Cacoqie Namuncura, who launched raids on the white settlers, burning their crops, killing their farm hands, and driving off their cattle. General Julio Roca and his forces decided to subdue the guerillas and captured 2,000 Araucanos — men, women, and children. Among the prisoners were the wife and four of the children of Cacique Namuncura, including Manuel Namuncura, Zeffirino's father. This was a decisive blow. The great chief had no choice but to surrender.

As this long tragedy was ending, Zeffirino (Zephyrin) Namuncura, the chief's grandson, was born in Chimpay, near the Black River, an area then blessed with the presence of Salvatorian missionaries. Fr. Domenico Milanesio (who had long been the only white man Chief Namuncura and his family trusted) baptized Zeffirino in 1888, two years after his birth.

Peace had already been restored at the time of Zeffirino's birth, so he grew up in a free and healthy environment. As a youngster he was a leader among his peers and was an excellent horseman, riding with great dexterity. With his brother, Anthony, he played and enjoyed the fresh air and the sun on the banks of the Black River.

At the age of eleven, Zeffirino asked permission of his parents to attend school so that he could be trained in ways that would be helpful to his tribe. The elders of the tribe held long discussions and finally, in 1897, decided that Zeffirino should go to study at the white men's school.

"You are the last hope of our tribe," he was told. "When you're grown up, you must defend the rights of the Araucano; otherwise, our tribe will be finished forever." Thus, Zefferino left his family to attend the government school of St. Fernando. Later he also attended the Salesian School of Pius IX in Buenos Aires.

He found a little difficulty at first with his white classmates, but he made great progress in his studies and soon became popular as well. He studied Christian doctrine with great interest and frequently attended church services. The headmaster of the school, noting his piety and great interest in prayer, soon arranged for Zeffirino's reception of his first Holy Communion on September 8, 1898, at the age of twelve.

The memory and the happiness of that day remained fervently in his heart for the rest of his life. His love of Jesus continued to grow, and he was fond of praying to the Blessed Mother under the title of "Help of Christians." His fervent and constant prayer at this time was "Jesus, please protect my brothers of the prairie." Then he would add apologetically, "If they don't love You, it is because they don't know you."

One day, after attending a conference given by Msgr. Cagliero, Zeffirino conferred with him about his desire to become a priest and a missionary among his people. The Monsignor was pleased with his request, since he had noticed the deep spirituality of the humble student. Even later, while Zeffirino was sent to the agricultural school of Uribelarrea, he wrote to Fr. Vespignani, reiterating his desire to follow his vocation. Zeffirino continued to pray for this intention while he grew in virtue and wisdom. His father had always hoped he would become a soldier or a politician who would be able to protect and help his people; however, he was resigned to anything that would make his son happy in life.

When Zeffirino was seventeen, he returned to school and began studying Latin. His classmates were enthralled by his tales of hunting and the stories of his grandfather, the great chief, who had finally dealt on even terms with the Argentine governor and the early white settlers. Excited by his stories, the younger boys made bows and arrows under his guidance and played in mock battles. When they grew weary, Zeffirino would lead them into the chapel for prayers.

Unfortunately, the Araucanos, robust in their own environment, now experienced health problems from their contact with the white men and were defenseless against germs and ordinary illnesses that they introduced. A common cold could quickly develop into pneumonia or fatal cases of tuberculosis, with victims in the thousands. Zefferino, though a picture of health, developed a stubborn and recurring cough. The priests at school decided he should return home for a time where he could breathe the thin, pure Andean air, but the cough persisted.

His continual plea to follow his vocation eventually started to become a reality. Msgr. Cagliero was named archbishop and planned on visiting Pope Pius X. With his father's consent, Zeffirino planned on going with him. In the company of Archbishop Cagliero, Zeffirino sailed for Turin where he met with Don Rua, the successor of St. Don Bosco. But he was especially pleased when he knelt before the great picture of Mary Help of Christians in her basilica, and before the tomb of Don Bosco in Valslice. In writing home he reassured his father, "Don't worry about me, I always have a doctor beside me to look after my health, and I'm always with my friend, Archbishop Cagliero."

This pious young Indian could never have imagined that he would someday meet the saintly Pope Pius X, but he did. In the company of Salesian priests, he traveled to Rome and spoke with the pope in perfect Italian, expressing to him his great desire, which the pope is said to have heard with "a happy interest." In the presence of many ecclesiastics, Zeffirino presented the pope with a handsome *quillango* made of skins by the Indians of his tribe. The pope received the gift with great pleasure and spoke words of encouragement regarding Zeffirino's priestly vocation.

At the Salesian school, he prayed and studied with great diligence. His fellow students, lively and exuberant Roman boys, had a deep respect for him. They saw him as a quiet and somewhat withdrawn young man. "I never saw him smile," recalled one of them. Another stated, "He was always serious, almost sad. Yet his eyes were always serene and smiling. In the chapel where he often went to pray, he was recollected like an angel." His school grades were excellent and his will to do good was enormous, but his health was growing progressively worse. It had been hoped that the warm climate and more advanced medicine in Italy might strengthen his condition, but Zeffirino's lungs had already been irreparably damaged by tuberculosis.

He returned to Turin and his studies, but Zeffirino could not acclimate himself to the raw winter weather, to which he was unaccustomed, and became seriously ill. Eventually his condition became critical. He was taken to the hospital on the Isola Tiberina in Rome, where he realized that he was going to die, and that his dream of becoming a priest would never come to pass. Nevertheless, he resigned himself to the will of God. After receiving the Holy Eucharist, assisted by his superior, he died on May 11, 1905.

In Argentina, a Salesian missionary informed the father of his son's death. The last hope of the Araucano Indians had vanished. Manuel Namuncura went outside, sat in front of his hut, and wept.

Zeffirino's body was returned to Argentina in 1924, where it rests at Fortin Mercedes, in the chapel where he had often prayed with fervor to the Madonna Auxiliatrice.

The Cause of his Beatification was introduced in 1945 and was deemed favorable by the presiding cardinals of the Sacred Congregation on December 11, 1956. Thus, the people of Argentina were delighted when their "Lily of the Prairie" was declared Venerable on June 22, 1972. ✝

Index of Saintly Youth

Occupations and Difficulties

P – R

Paralysis -
Aldo Blundo, 15
Alexia Gonzalez-Barros, 23
Bernard Lehner, 70
Chiara Luce Badano, 76
Maria Cristina Ogier, 157
Paratyphoid -
Anne de Guigne, 47
Phlebitis -
Faustino Perez-Manglano, 86
Mari Carmen Gonzlez-Valerio,
140
Pleurisy -
Aldo Blundo, 15
Maggiorino Vigolungo, 134
Stephen Kaszap, 207
Pneumonia -
Aldo Blundo, 15
Francisco Marto, 95
Zeffirino Namuncura, 212
Pott's disease -
Ramon Montero Navarro, 189
Priestly vocation aspired to -
Faustino Perez-Manglano, 84
Maggiorino Vigolungo, 134
Zeffirino Namuncura, 212-213
Printer - Maggiorino Vigolungo,
133
Prisoner, political -
José Sánchez del Rio, 117
Progressive degenerate myopia -
Aldo Blundo, 15
Prosthesis worn -
Lorena D'Alexander, 131

S

Scapular
devotee - Maria Carmelina
Leone, 144
martyr - Isidore Bakanja, 107

Scarlet fever -
Mari Carmen Gonzalez-Valerio,
140
Septicemia -
Mari Carmen Gonzalez-Valerio,
140
Sewing -
Maria Carmelina Leone, 144
Maria Lichtenegger, 165
Montserrat Grases, 174
Shepherd -
Francisco Marto, 90-91
Jacinta Marto, 110-115
Society of St. Paul -
Maggiorino Vigolungo, 134
Sodality of the Children of Mary -
Laura Vicuña, 127
Spinal column damage -
Alexia Gonzalez-Barros, 22

T – Z

Tailor -
Maria Carmelina Leone, 144
Teacher -
Paula Renata Carboni, 182
Throat difficulties -
Aldo Blundo, 15
Antonietta Meo, 68
Stephen Kaszap, 209
Thrombectomy -
Mari Carmen Gonzalez-Valero,
140
Tonsillitis -
Antonietta Meo, 63
Lorena D'Alexander, 130
Stephen Kaszap, 207
Traction -
Alexia Gonzalez-Barros, 22
Tuberculosis -
Angelina Pirini, 36
Annie Zelikova, 51

Selected Bibliography

A Benedictine Nun of Stanbrook Abbey. *Anne, The Life of Venerable Anne De Guigne*. TAN Books and Publishers, Inc. Rockford, Illinois. 1997.

Agli Amici di Silvio Dissegna, Morto di Cancro a 12 Anni. Special Issue for the Diocesan Process. Edito dall'Associazione "Amici di Silvio." Turin. 2002.

Amati, Giordano, Bruno Benini, Mario Morigi, Angelo Pirini. *Prendere Il Largo . . . Con Angelina*. Stilgraf di Cesena. 2002.

Amati, Giordano, Bruno Benini, Valentino Maraldi. *Angelina Docile Allo Spirito*. Stilgraf di Cesena. 1998.

Anfrosina Berardi, Serva di Dio. Paper.

Bibliotheca Sanctorum. Citta' Nuova Editrice. Rome, Italy. 1987.

Boday, S.J., Jeno. *Stephen Kaszap, Servant of God*.

Borriello, L., Caruana, E., Del Genio, M.R., Suffi, N. *Dizionario Di Mistica*. Libreria Editrice Vaticana. Rome, Italy. No date.

Cejas, José Miguel. *Montse, A fun-loving teenager*. Scepter. London, England. 1994.

Cirrincione, Msgr. Joseph A. *Venerable Jacinta Marto of Fátima*. TAN Books and Publishers, Inc. Rockford, Illinois. 1992.

Convento Madonna della Misericordia Agostiniani Scalzi. *Venerable Paola Renata Carboni*. Paper. Fermo, Italy.

Cruz, Joan Carroll. *Secular Saints*. Tan Books and Publishers. Rockford, Illinois. 1989.

D'Amando, Filippo. *Una Mistica Motorizzata, Carla Ronci*. Editrice Elle Dl Cl. Turin, Italy. 1989.

De Giorgi, Salvatore. *Il Vangelo Dei Bambini*. Editrice. Rome, Italy. 1955.

Eguibar, Mercedes. *Montserrat Grases, Una Vida Sencilla*. Cuarta Edicion. Madrid, Spain. 1967.

Fátima in Lucia's Own Words, Sister Lucia's Memoirs. Postulation Centre. Fátima, Portugal. 1976.

Fortunato, P. Passionista. *La Beata Antonia Mesina*. Giovane di Azione Cattolica Uccisa per la Sua Purezza. Nettuno, Italy. No date.

Girardi, S.C.J., P. Giuseppe. *Antonietta Meo accanto alla croce*. Apostolato della Riparazione. Bologna, Italy. 1962.

Il Messaggio di Laura Vicuña. Congregazione Salesiana. Turin, Italy. 1971. August, 1997.

Leite, S.J., Father Fernando. *Francisco of Fátima, Our Lady's Little Shepherd.* Vice-Postulation of the Little Shepherds. Fátima, Portugal. 1980.

Lorena D'Alessandro, *Una giovinezza offerta a Dio.* Leaflet. Fabriano. 1964.

Madden, Daniel. *A Brief Account of the Life of Blessed Laura Vicuña.* The Salesian Missions. New Rochelle, New York. 1999.

Maraldi, Valentino. *Angelina, La Sua Vita E L'Eucaristia.*

Maria Carmelina Leone E Venerabile. Leaflet. Palermo.

Maurus of Mary Immaculate, C.P., Fr. *The Martyr of le Ferriere, St. Mary Goretti.* Scala Santa. Rome, Italy. No date.

Medeiros, Rev. Humberto S. and Rev. William F. Hill. *Jacinta, The Flower of Fátima.* Catholic Book Publishing Company. New York, New York. 1946.

Mondrone, S.J., Domenico. *Angiolino, Un Ragazzo Che Seppe Soffrire.* Centro Volontari Della Sofferenza. Rome. 1992.

Montserrat Graces, The Servant of God. Office of Vice Postulator of Opus Dei in the Philippines. New Manila, The Philippines. 1997.

Moscone, Felice. *Angiolino Bonetta, Sono tutto della Madonna: dalla testa ai piedi.* C.V.S. Roma. 1998.

Moser, SDB., Dom Hilario, Bispo de Tubarao. A Serva de Deus, Albertina Berkenbrock. Livraria N. Sra. Da Piedade. Tubarao, Brazil. 2001.

Myriam de G. *Fiaccola Romana, Antonietta Meo (Nennolina).* Roberto Berruti a.c. Turin, Italy. No date.

Quintas, P. Alfonso Lopez. *Pilina Cimadevilla y Lopez-Doriga, Enferma Misionera.* Madrid, Spain. 1963.

Rachelina Ambrosini, Una Ragazza Vissuta per il Cielo. Fondazione Rachelin Ambrosini. Venticano, Italy.

Rachelina Ambrosini, La Serva di Dio, Il Giglio d'Irpinia. Per la chiusura del "Processo Diocesano." Benevento, 1995.

Rachelina Ambrosini, A Girl Who Lived for Heaven. Fondazione Rachelina Ambrosini. Venticano (AV), Italy.

Risso, Paolo. *Silvio Dissegna, Un Ragazzo Meraviglioso.* Editrice Elledici. Turin. 2002.

Rossi, C.M., Amedeo. *Antonietta Meo (Nennolina), Studio Biografico.* Tip. Le. Company. Piacenza, Italy. 1986.

Salaverri, José Maria. *Tal vez me hable Dios.* Ediciones S.M. Madrid, Spain. 1986.

Salaverri, José Maria. *Maybe God Will Speak to Me, the Story of Faustino Perez-Manglano*. Valencia, Spain. 1993.

Salaverri, José Maria. *The Four Yeses of Faustino.*

Sanchez, Adolfo Olivera. *Rotos los Huesos, entera el alma. Pilina Cimadevilla, La sierva de Dios de diez anos*. Sociedad de Educacion Atenas. Madrid, Spain. No date.

Sbriscia, S., Vannini, F., Bertelli, V.G., Moretti, R., Carriguiry, G., Calabrese, G., Giusti, S., Ciccone, L. *Il Vangelo Dei Bambini*. Editrice Ave. Rome, Italy. 1995.

Servant of God Montserrat Grases. Office of the Vice Postulation of Opus Dei in the United States. New York, New York. 1999.

Servant of God Montserrat Grases. Informative Bulletin #2. Office of Vice Postulation of Opus Dei in the Philippines. New Manila, Quezon City, The Philippines. August 1997.

Setti, Mons. Giancarlo. *In the Light of the Epiphany, Maria Cristina Ogier*. Italy. 1977.

Silvestrelli, p. Stef. Igino. *Brigante No! Profilo Biografico di Maggiorino Vigolungo Venerabile*. Edizioni Casa Di Nazareth. Roma. 1988.

Valabek, O.Carm., Fr. Redemptus Maria. *Carmel's Youth Candidate: Santos Franco Sanchez. Carmel in the World*. Rome, Italy. Vol. XXXIII, Number 3. 1994.

Valabek, O.Carm., Fr. Redemptus Maria. "Annie Zelikova." *Profiles in Holiness I*. Edizioni Carmelitane. Rome, Italy. 1996.

Valabek, O.Carm., Fr. Redemptus Maria. "Carmel's Youth Candidate, Santos Franco Sanchez." *Profiles in Holiness II*. Edizioni Carmelitane. Rome, Italy. 1999.

Valabek, O.Carm., Fr. Redemptus Maria. "The Boy from La Mancha, Ramon Montero Navarro." *Profiles in Holiness II*. Edizioni Carmelitane. Rome, Italy. 1999.

Vanzan, Piersandro. *Antonietta Meo piccola evangelista della sofferenza*. Nuova Responsabilita. Febbraio, 2000.

Verd-Conradi, S.J., Gabriel M. *Mari Carmen Gonzalez-Valerio, A Girl on Her Way to the Altars*. Madres Carmelitas Descalzas. Madrid, Spain. 1993.

Zanzucchi, Mike. *Chiara Luce, Sanctity in 18 years*. New City Publications. Volume XXXV, No. 6, June 2000.

Our Sunday Visitor …
Your Source for Discovering
the Riches of the Catholic Faith

Our Sunday Visitor has an extensive line of materials for young children, teens, and adults. Our books, Bibles, pamphlets, CD-ROMs, audios, and videos are available in bookstores worldwide.

To receive a FREE full-line catalog or for more information, call **Our Sunday Visitor** at **1-800-348-2440, ext. 3**. Or write **Our Sunday Visitor** / 200 Noll Plaza / Huntington, IN 46750.

Please send me ___ A catalog
Please send me materials on:
___ Apologetics and catechetics
___ Prayer books
___ The family
___ Reference works
___ Heritage and the saints
___ The parish

Name _____
Address _____ Apt._____
City _____ State _____ Zip_____
Telephone (   ) _____
                                          A63BBBBP

Please send a friend ___ A catalog
Please send a friend materials on:
___ Apologetics and catechetics
___ Prayer books
___ The family
___ Reference works
___ Heritage and the saints
___ The parish

Name _____
Address _____ Apt._____
City _____ State _____ Zip_____
Telephone (   ) _____
                                          A63BBBBP

OurSundayVisitor

200 Noll Plaza, Huntington, IN 46750
Toll free: **1-800-348-2440**
Website: www.osv.com